BRAC

AUTHENTIC TRANSCRIPTIONS
WITH NOTES AND TABLATURE

John Mellencamp
GUITAR COLLECTION

Cover photo by Kurt Markus

Music transcriptions by Pete Billmann and Steve Gorenberg

ISBN 978-0-634-03304-9

CORPORATION

7777 W. BLUEMOUND RD. P.O. BOX 13819 MILWAUKEE, WI 53213

Visit Hal Leonard Online at
www.halleonard.com

Ain't Even Done With the Night

Words and Music by John Mellencamp

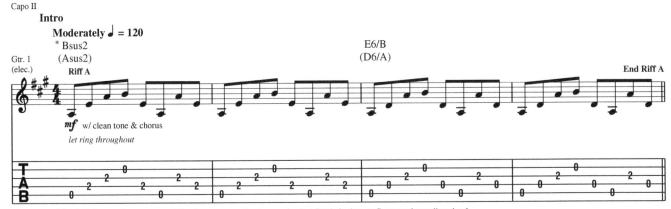

* Symbols in parentheses represent chord names respective to capoed guitar. Symbols above reflect actual sounding chord.
  Capoed fret is "0" in tab. Chord symbols reflect overall harmony.

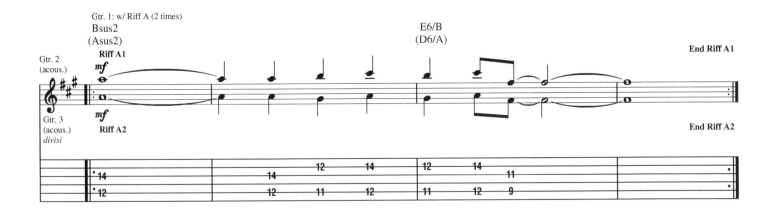

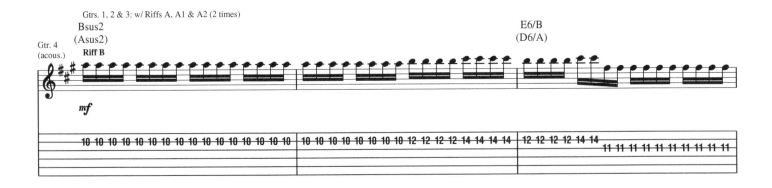

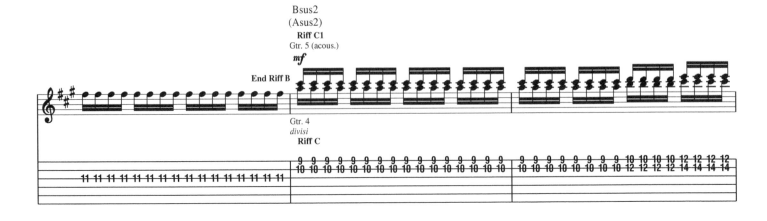

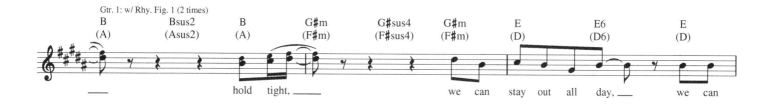

hold tight, _____ we can stay out all day, _____ we can

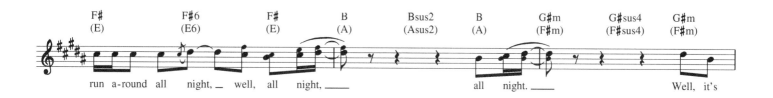

run a-round all night, _ well, all night, _____ all night. _____ Well, it's

To Coda ⊕

1.

Interlude
Gtrs. 1, 2 & 3: w/ Riffs A, A1 & A2 (2 times)
Gtr. 4: w/ Riff B

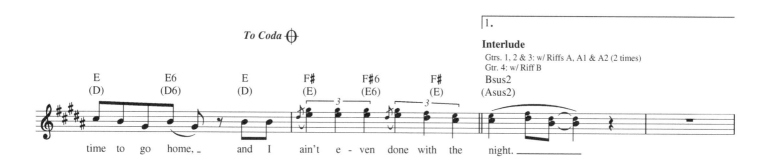

time to go home, _ and I ain't e - ven done with the night. _____

Gtrs. 4 & 5: w/ Riffs C & C1

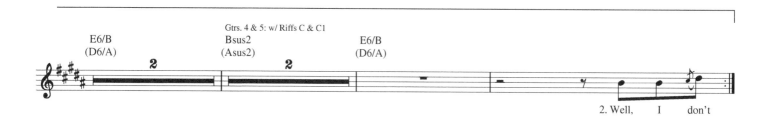

2. Well, I don't

2.

Saxophone Solo

night. _____

Gtr. 1

7

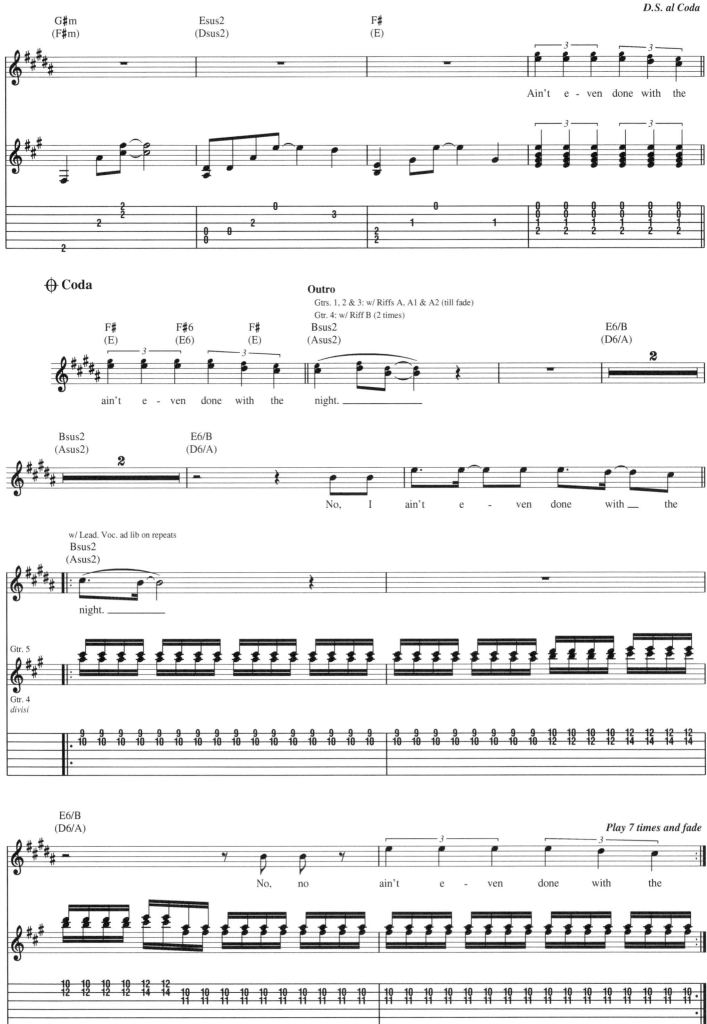

Authority Song

Words and Music by John Mellencamp

Double drop D tuning:
(low to high) D–A–D–G–B–D

Intro

Moderately fast Rock ♩ = 157

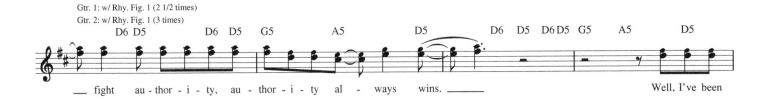

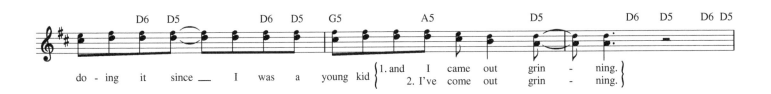

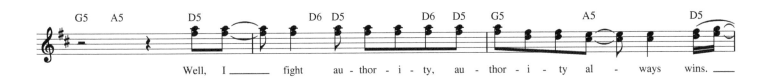

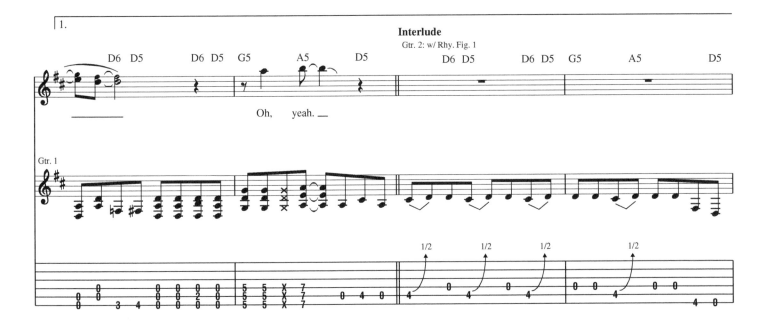

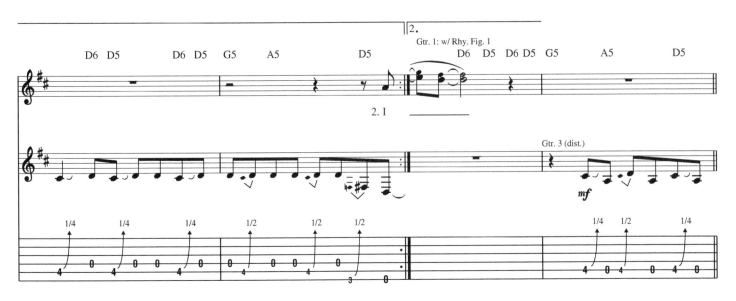

Guitar Solo

* Refers to upstemmed vocs. only.

Check It Out

Words and Music by John Mellencamp

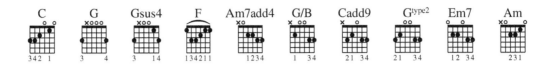

Intro

Moderate Rock ♩ = 108

*Banjo arr. for gtr.

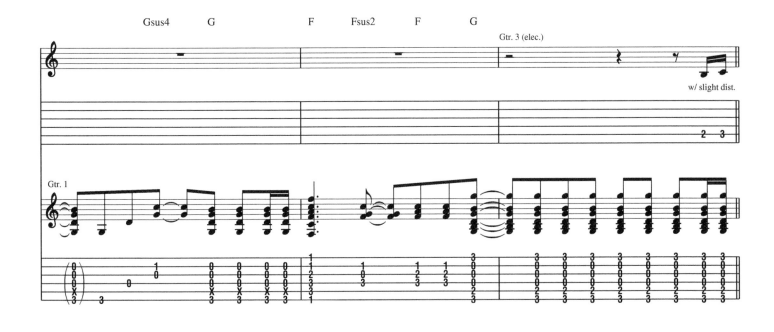

Interlude

Guitar Solo

*Composite arrangement.

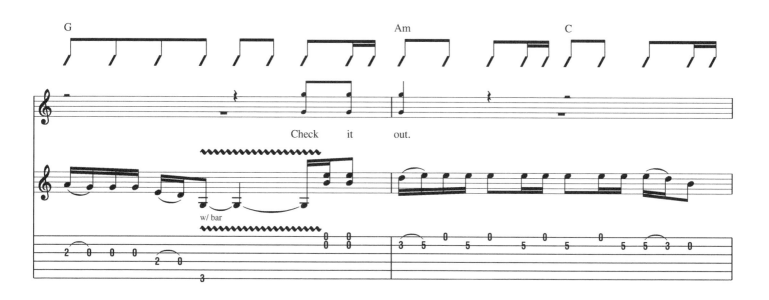

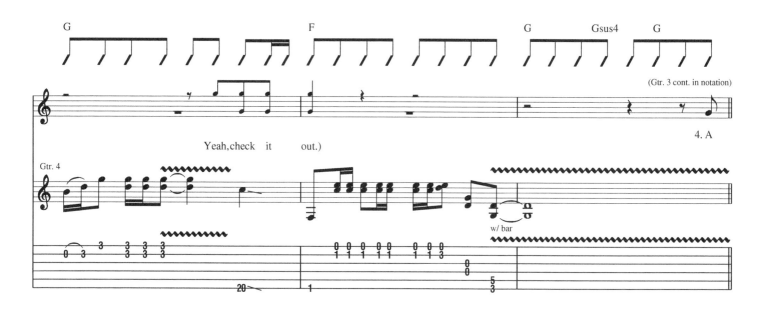

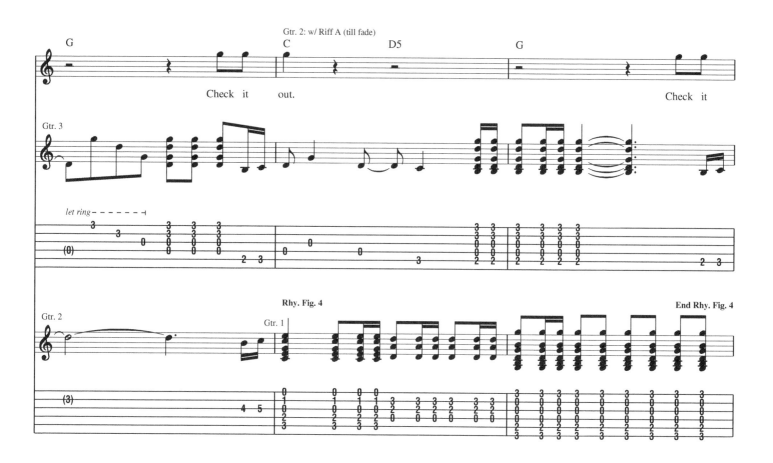

Cherry Bomb

Words and Music by John Mellencamp

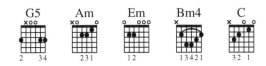

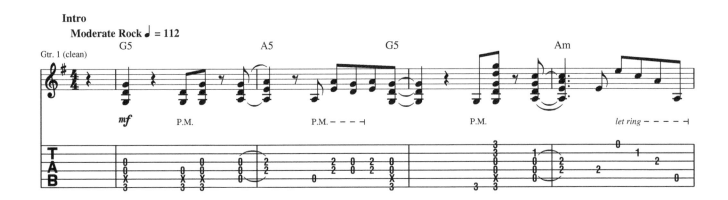

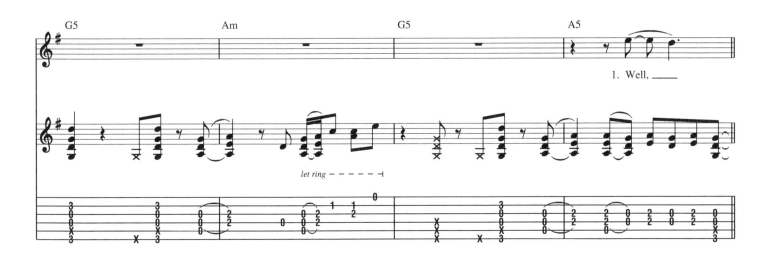

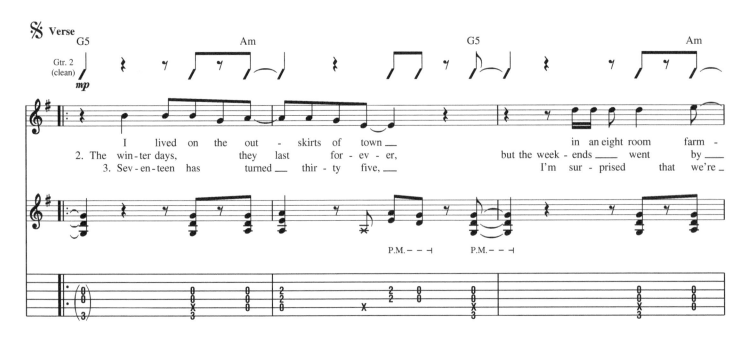

Crumblin' Down

Words and Music by John Mellencamp and George Green

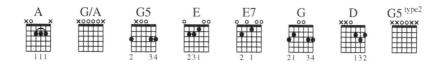

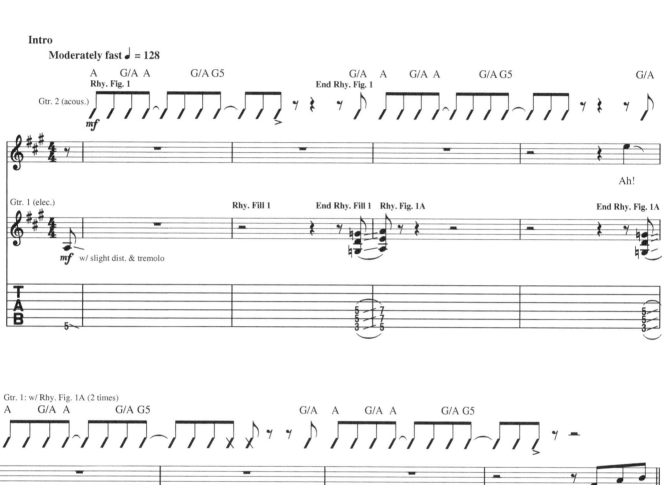

deed goes un - pun - ished. And I don't mind _____ be - ing their _____
pin - ion means noth - in'. But I know _____ I'm a

_____ whip - ping boy. _____ I've had _____ that pleas - ure for
real good danc - er. Don't need to look o - ver my shoul - der to

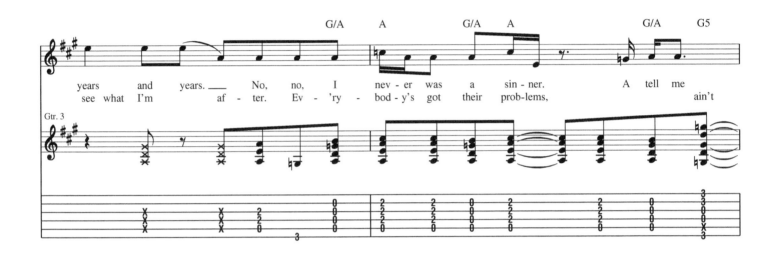

years and years. _____ No, no, I nev - er was a sin - ner. A tell me
see what I'm af - ter. Ev - 'ry - bod - y's got their prob - lems, ain't

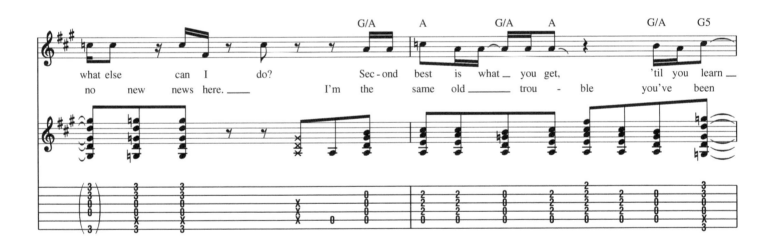

what else can I do? Sec - ond best is what ___ you get, 'til you learn _____
no new news here. _____ I'm the same old _____ trou - ble you've been

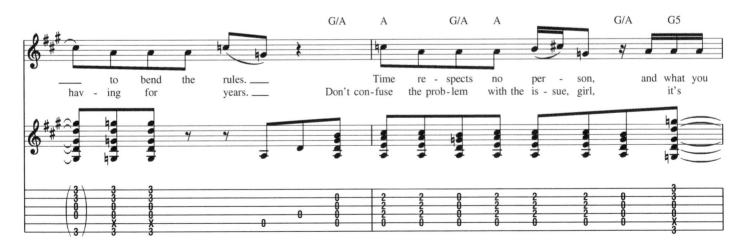

_____ to bend the rules. _____ Time re - spects no per - son, and what you
hav - ing for years. _____ Don't con - fuse the prob - lem with the is - sue, girl, it's

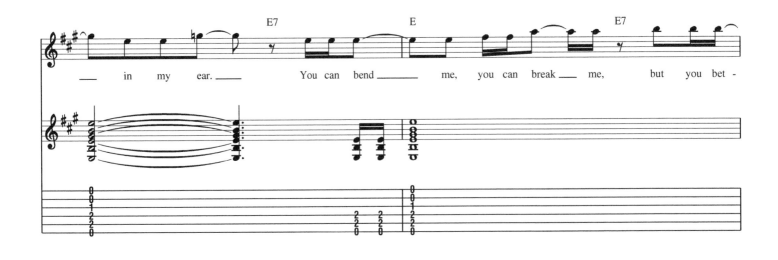

Chorus
w/ Lead. Voc. ad lib on repeat

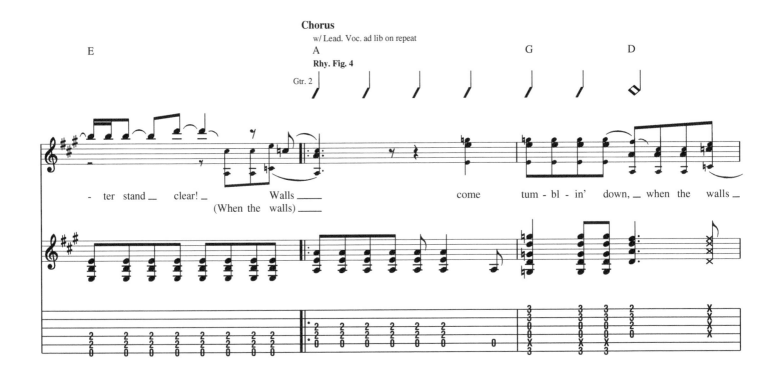

Dance Naked

Words and Music by John Mellencamp

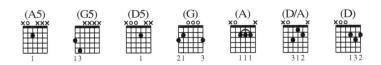

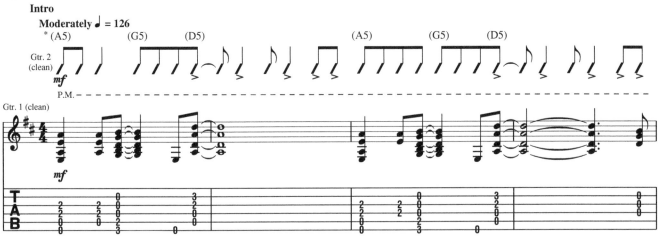

* Symbols in parentheses represent chord names respective to capoed guitar and do not reflect actual sounding chord.

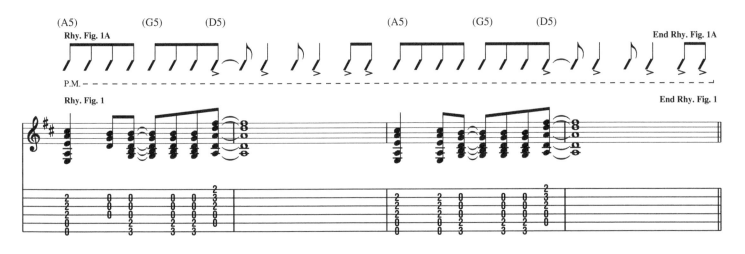

Verse

1st time, Gtrs. 1 & 2: w/ Rhy. Figs. 1 & 1A (2 times)
2nd time, Gtr. 1: w/ Rhy. Fig. 3 (4 times)
2nd time, Gtr. 2: w/ Rhy. Fig. 1A (2 times)

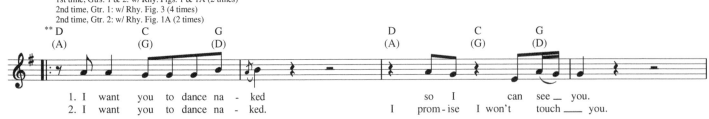

1. I want you to dance na - ked
2. I want you to dance na - ked.

so I can see __ you.
I prom - ise I won't touch __ you.

** Symbols in parentheses represent chord names respective to capoed guitar.
Symbols above reflect actual sounding chord. Capoed fret is "0" in tab.

I'd like to get to know __ you.
I prom - ise to tell no one, no,

You don't have to act naugh -
I want you to dance na -

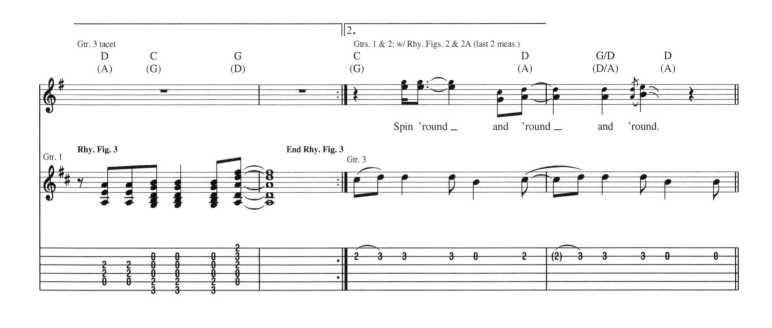

Spin 'round __ and 'round __ and 'round.

Verse

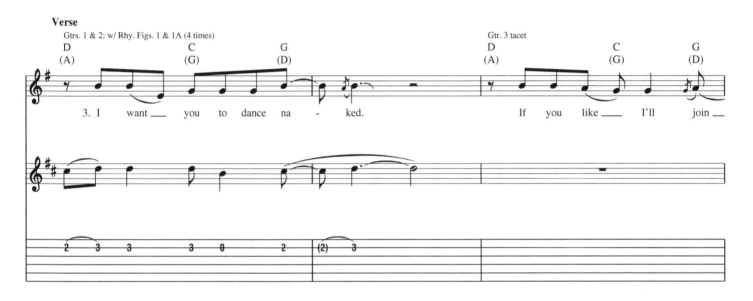

3. I want __ you to dance na - ked. If you like __ I'll join

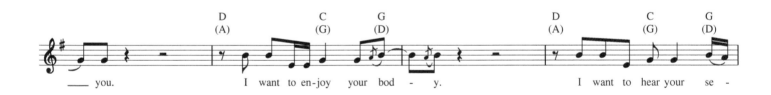

__ you. I want to en-joy your bod - y. I want to hear your se -

crets. I want to know if you like __ me __ as much as I __ like you. __

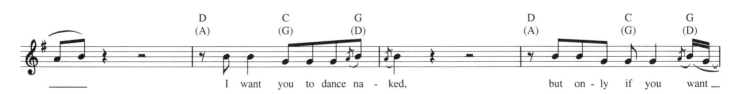

_____ I want you to dance na - ked, but on - ly if you want __

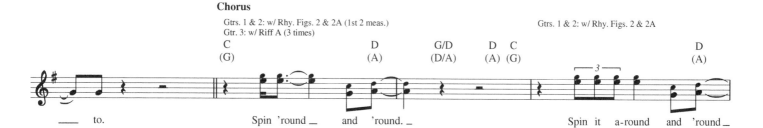

Chorus

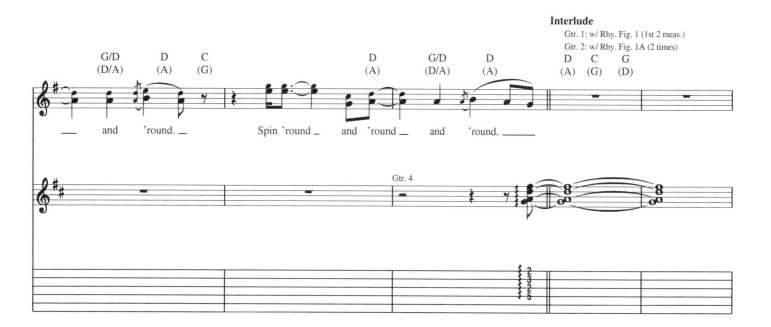

Interlude

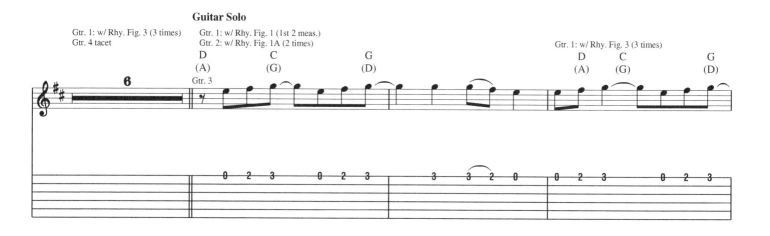

Guitar Solo

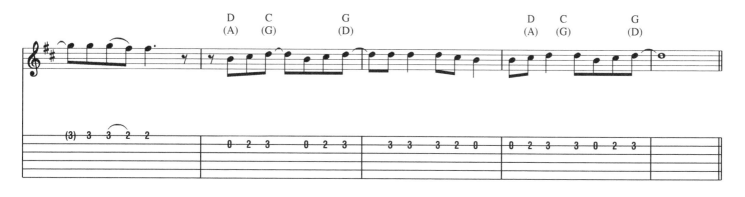

Verse

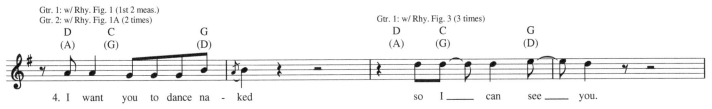

Chorus

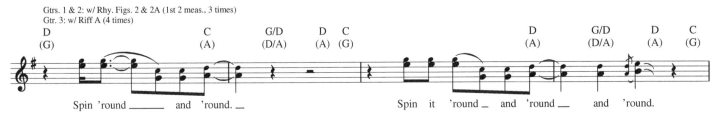

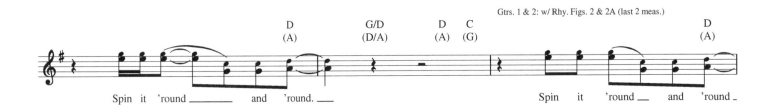

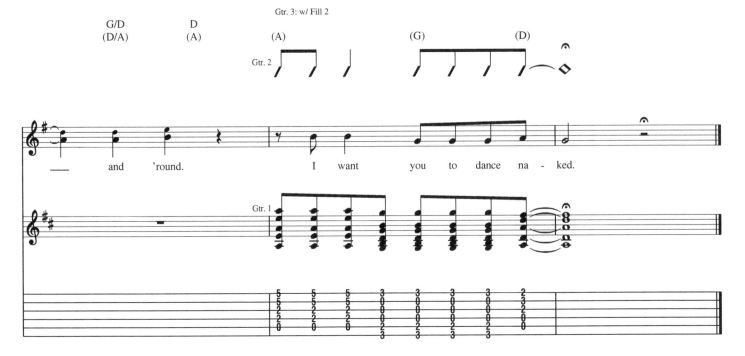

Hurts So Good

Words and Music by John Mellencamp and George Green

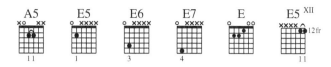

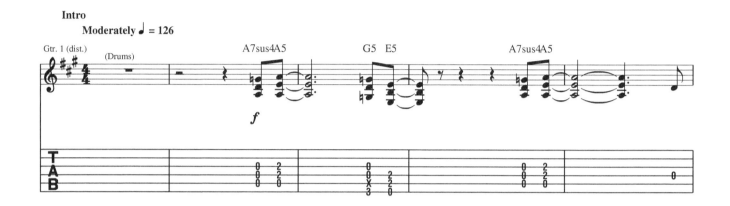

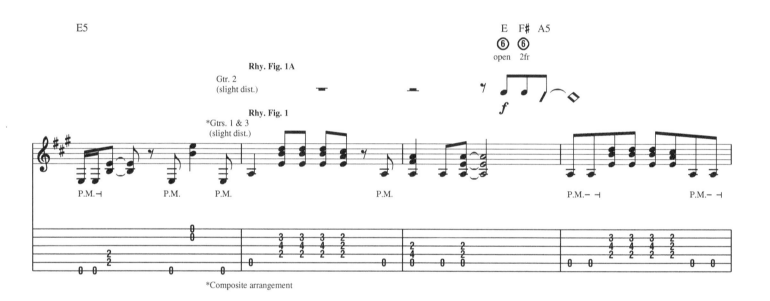

*Composite arrangement

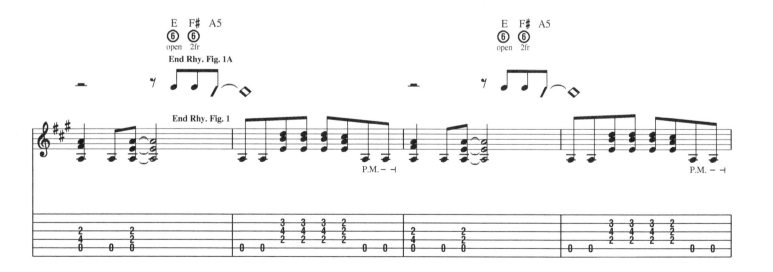

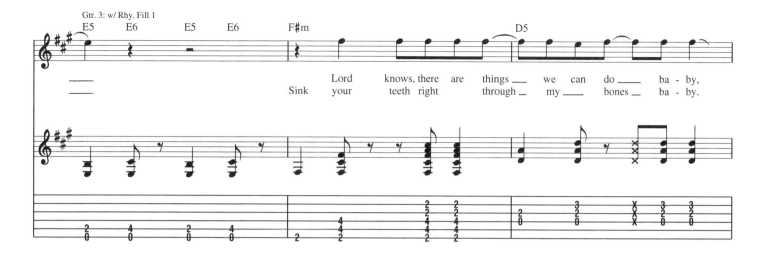

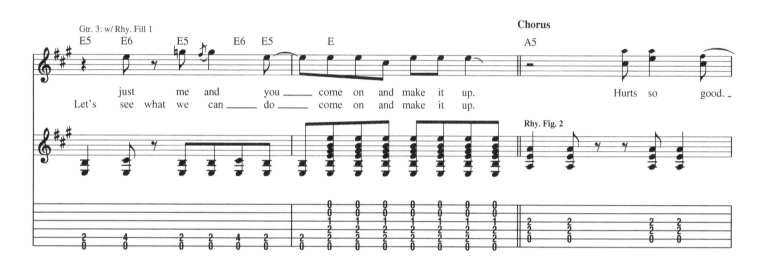

46

Chorus

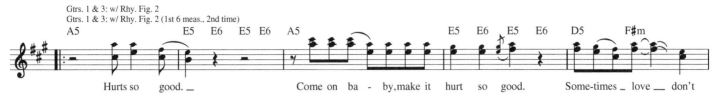

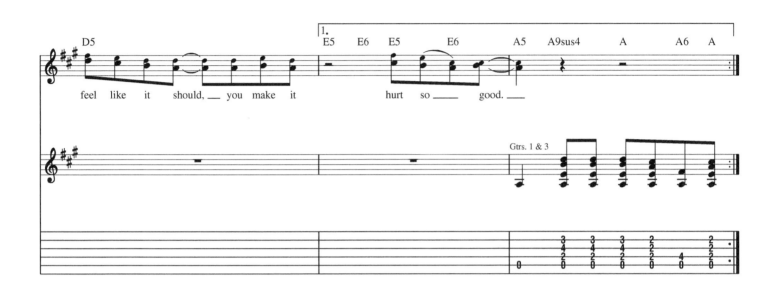

Outro

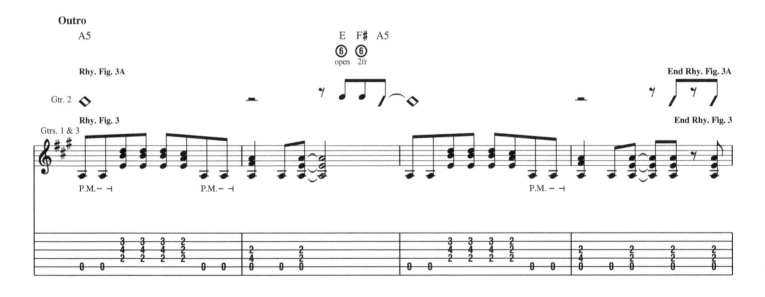

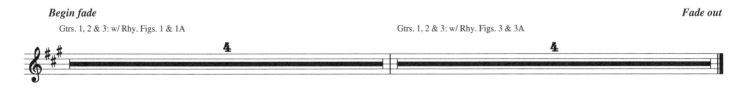

I Need a Lover

Words and Music by John Mellencamp

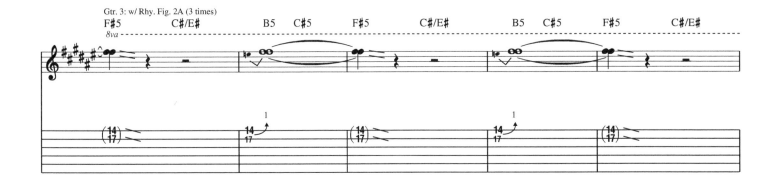

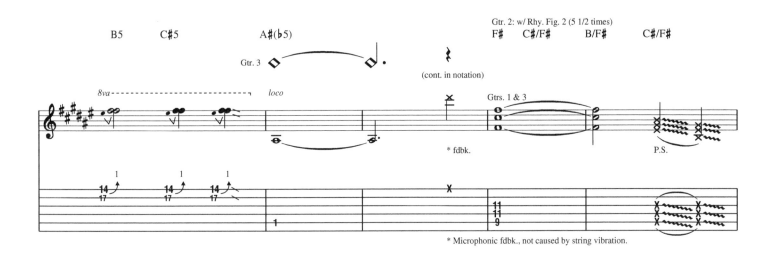

* Microphonic fdbk., not caused by string vibration.

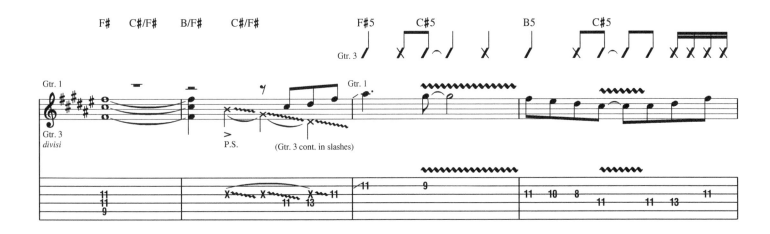

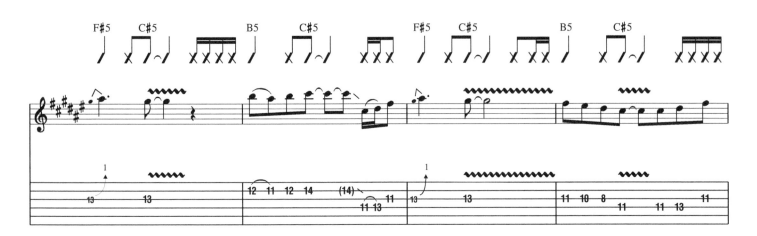

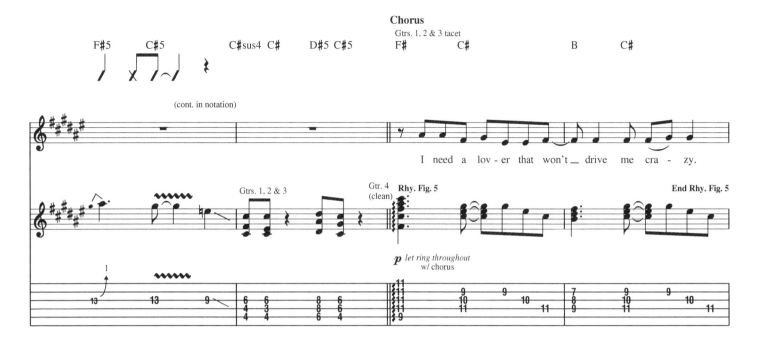

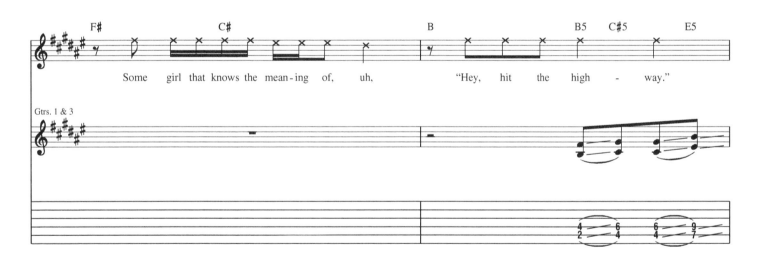

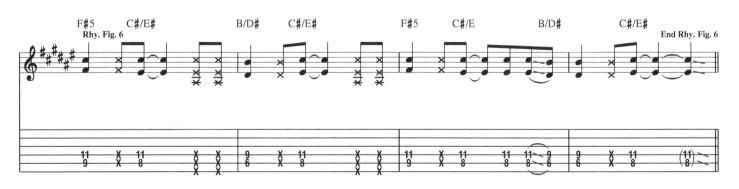

Verse

Gtr. 4: w/ Rhy. Fig. 5 (4 times)
Gtrs. 1 & 3 tacet

1. Well, I've been walk-ing the streets __ up and down, rac - ing through __ the hu-man jun-

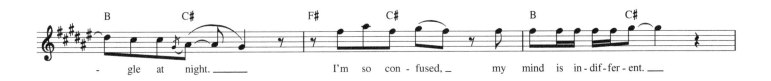

- gle at night. _____ I'm so con - fused, __ my mind is in-dif-fer-ent. ___

Hey, I'm __ so weak, won't some-bod - y shut off that light. ____ Ow!

Gtr. 3

* Push 6th string behind nut.

Gtrs. 1 & 3: w/ Rhy. Fig. 6

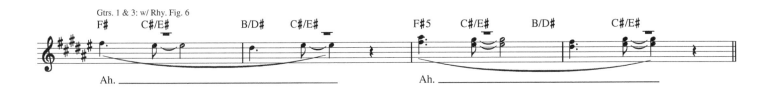

Ah. _____ Ah. _____

Verse

Gtr. 4: w/ Rhy. Fig. 5 (3 1/2 times)

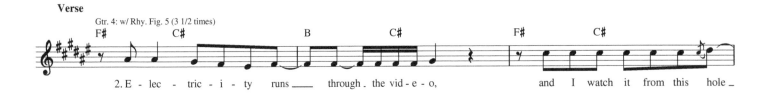

2. E - lec - tric - i - ty runs __ through . the vid - e - o, and I watch it from this hole __

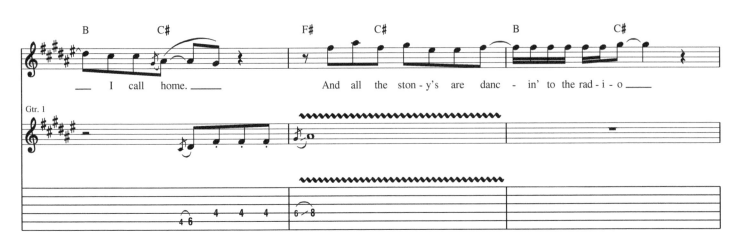

__ I call home. ___ And all the ston - y's are danc - in' to the rad - i - o __

Gtr. 1

and I got the world _ call-ing me up _ here _ to - night _ on the phone. _____

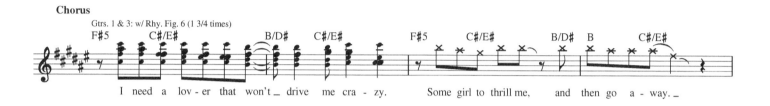

Chorus

I need a lov - er that won't _ drive me cra - zy. Some girl to thrill me, and then go a - way. _

I need a lov - er that won't _ drive me cra - zy. Some girl that knows the mean-ing of uh,

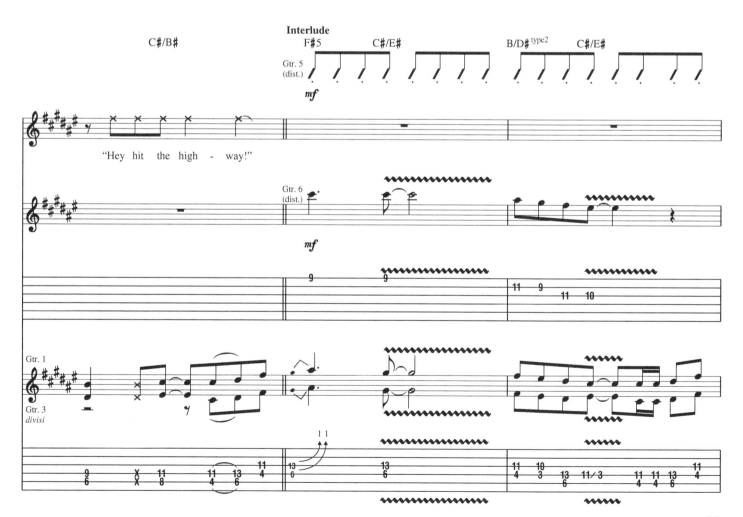

"Hey hit the high - way!"

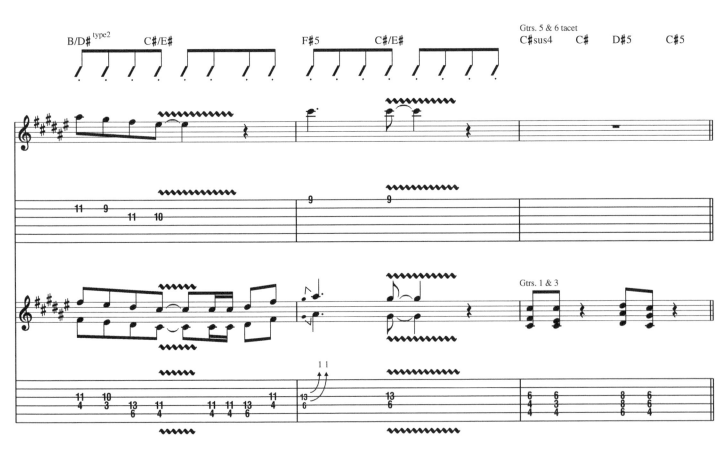

Verse

Gtr. 4: w/ Rhy. Fig. 5 (3 1/2 times)
Gtr. 1 & 3 tacet

3. Well, I'm___ not wiped out by this pool-room life ___ I'm liv - ing. ___   I'm gon-na quit this job, go to school ___

or head back home. _____ And I'm _ not ask-ing to be loved _ or be for-giv-en.

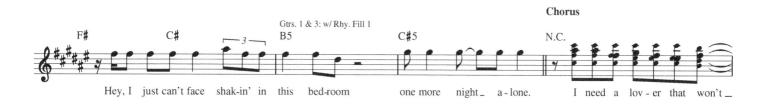

Hey, I just can't face shak-in' in this bed-room one more night_ a-lone. I need a lov-er that won't _

_ drive me cra - zy. I need a lov-er that won't _ drive me cra - zy.

I need a lov-er that won't _ drive me cra - zy. Some girl that knows the mean-ing of uh,

"Hey hit the high - way!"

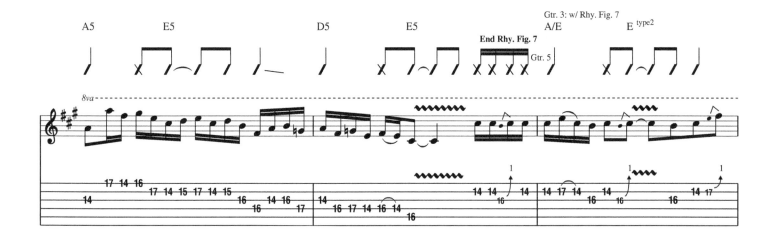

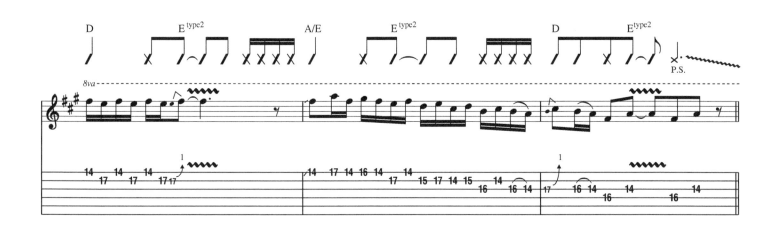

Chorus

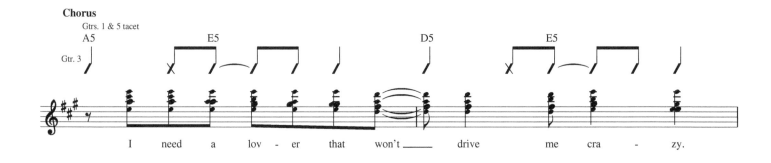

I need a lov - er that won't _____ drive me cra - zy.

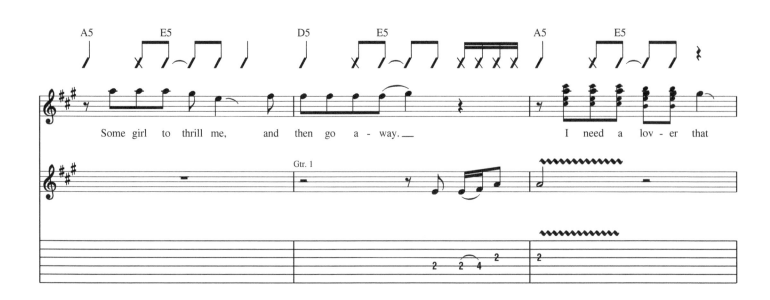

Some girl to thrill me, and then go a - way. ___ I need a lov - er that

won't drive me cra - zy. Some girl that knows the mean - ing of uh,

"Hey hit the high - way!" You bet ya.

(cont. in notation)

Jack and Diane

Words and Music by John Mellencamp

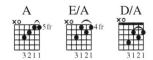

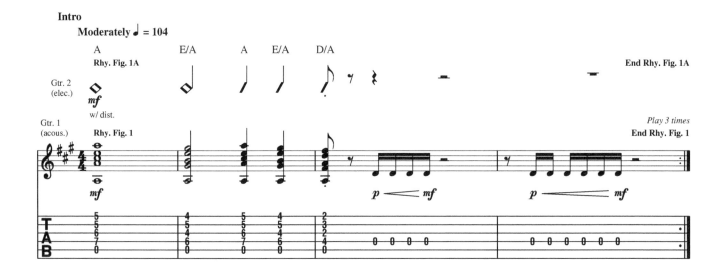

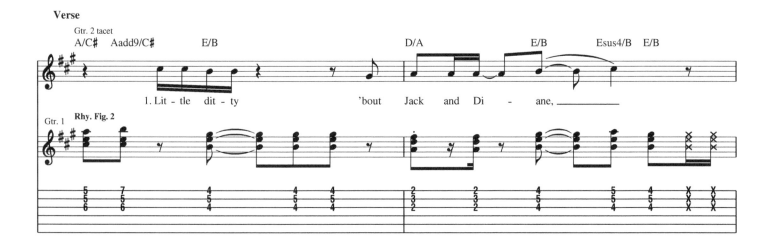

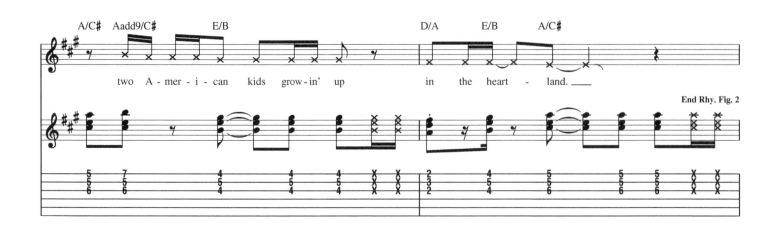

long af - ter the thrill of liv - in' is ___ gone. ___ Oh, yeah, ___ I say life ___

Gtr. 1: w/ Rhy. Fig. 2 (last 2 meas.)

___ goes _ on ___ long af - ter the thrill of liv - in' is ___ gone. ___

Outro

A lit - tle dit - ty 'bout Jack and Di - ane. ___

two A - mer - i - can kids do - in' ___ best they _ can. ___

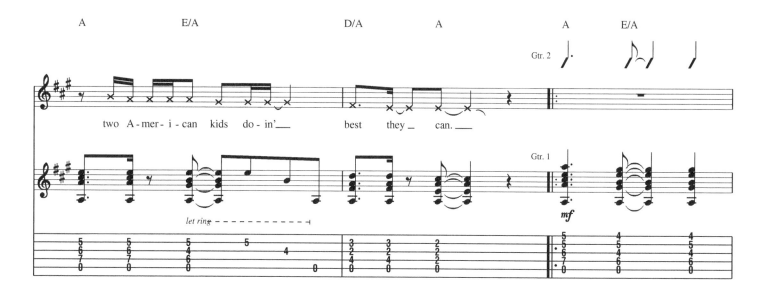

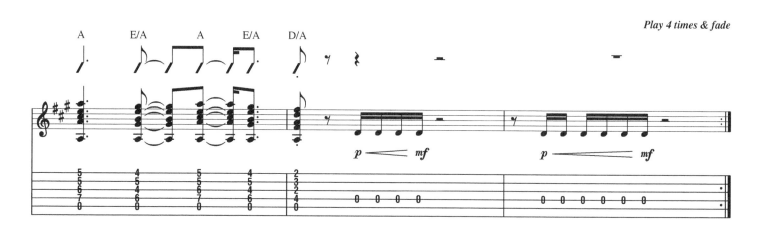

Play 4 times & fade

Just Another Day

Words and Music by John Mellencamp

* Symbols in parentheses represent chord names (implied harmony) respective to capoed guitar.
  Symbols above reflect actual sounding chord. Capoed fret is "0" in tab.

Interlude

Verse

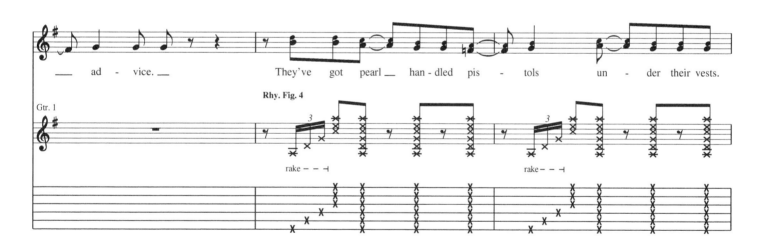

⊕ Coda

Interlude

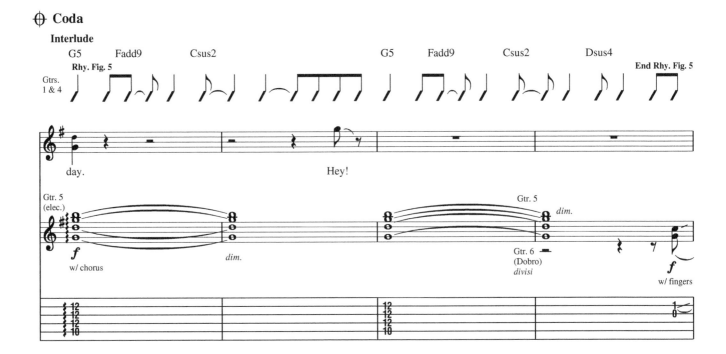

day.　　　　　　　　　　　Hey!

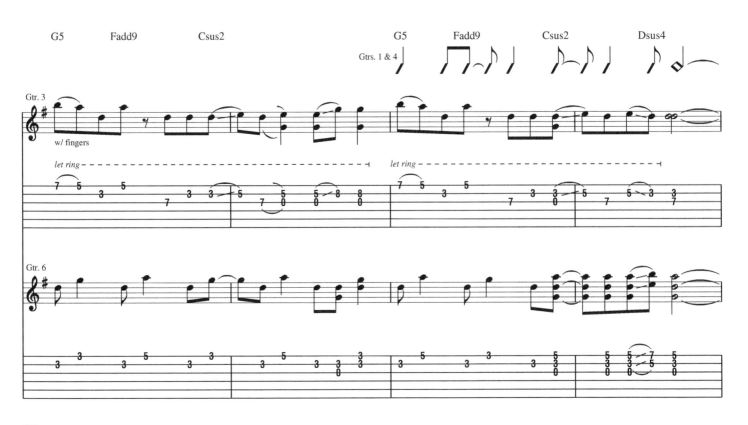

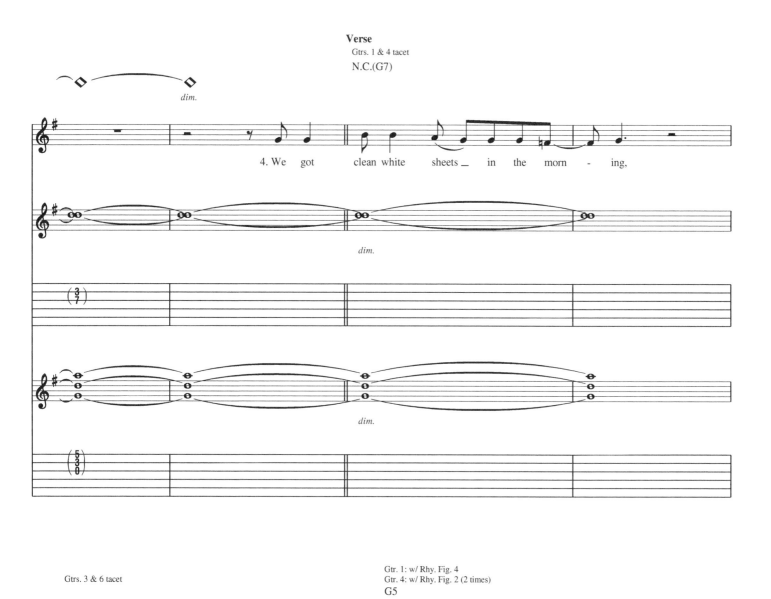

Verse

Gtrs. 1 & 4 tacet

N.C.(G7)

4. We got clean white sheets ___ in the morn - ing,

dim.

Gtrs. 3 & 6 tacet

con - ver - sa - tion all af - ter - noon. ___

Gtr. 1: w/ Rhy. Fig. 4
Gtr. 4: w/ Rhy. Fig. 2 (2 times)

G5

Bo - bie Doll ___ and Big ___ Jim Pi - ca - to, ba - by,

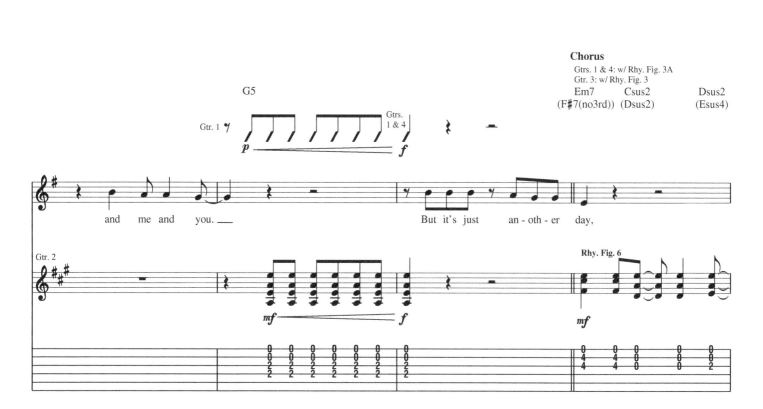

G5

Chorus

Gtrs. 1 & 4: w/ Rhy. Fig. 3A
Gtr. 3: w/ Rhy. Fig. 3

Em7   Csus2   Dsus2
(F♯7(no3rd)) (Dsus2)   (Esus4)

and me and you. ___

But it's just an - oth - er day,

Rhy. Fig. 6

Gtr. 2

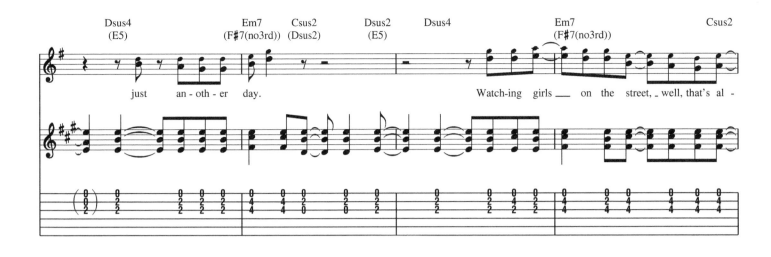

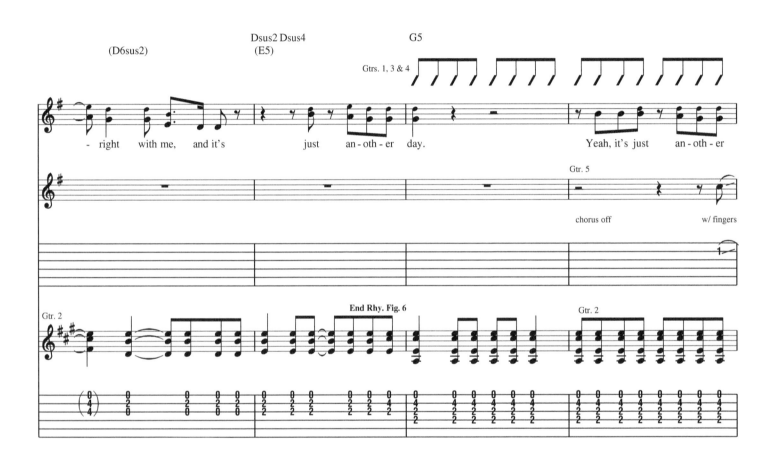

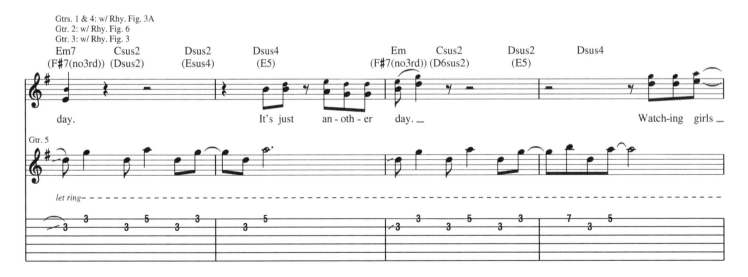

Key West Intermezzo (I Saw You First)

Words and Music by John Mellencamp and George M. Green

Gtr. 1: Capo II
Gtr. 2: Capo IV

Intro

Moderately ♩ = 116

Verse
Gtr. 3 tacet

*F#maj7add4
**(Emaj7add4)
†((Dmaj7add4))

F#maj7add4
(Emaj7add4)
((Dmaj7add4))

*Chord symbols reflect overall harmony.
**Symbols in parentheses represent chord names respective to capoed Gtr. 1.
Symbols above reflect actual sounding chords. Capoed fret is "0" in tab.
†Symbols in double parentheses represent chord names respective to capoed Gtr. 2.

She could be danc - ing with ___ me.

Gtr. 2: w/ Rhy. Fig. 3

Gtr. 2: w/ Rhy. Fig. 2A
Gtr. 3: w/ Riff A1

G#m
(F#m)
((Em))

F#maj7add4
(Emaj7add4)
((Dmaj7add4))

She stirs the ice in her glass ___ with her el - e - gant fin - ger.

Gtr. 1

Gtr. 2: w/ Rhy. Fig. 3

Gtr. 2: w/ Rhy. Fig. 2A
Gtrs. 1 & 3: w/ Riffs A & A1

G#m
(F#m)
((Em))

F#maj7add4
(Emaj7add4)
((Dmaj7add4))

I want to be what she's drink - ing, yeah, I just want ___ to ___ be. ___

Chorus

((G5))   ((D))   ((Em))   ((D))

Rhy. Fig. 4A   End Rhy. Fig. 4A

Gtr. 2

I ___ saw you first. ___ I'm the first one ___ to - night. ___

Gtr. 1   Rhy. Fig. 4   End Rhy. Fig. 4

Gtr. 1: w/ Rhy. Fig. 4
Gtr. 2: w/ Rhy. Fig. 4A (1 3/4 times)

Bsus2 (Asus2) ((Gsus2)) F# (E) ((D)) G#m7add4 (F#m7add4) ((Em7add4)) F# (E) ((D))

I ___ saw you first. ___ Don't __ that give me ___ the right ___

Bsus2 (Asus2) ((Gsus2)) F# (E) ((D)) G#m7add4 (F#m7add4) ((Em7add4)) ((A7sus4))

Gtr. 2

to move _ a - round __ in your heart? Ev'-ry-one was look - ing but I saw you

Gtr. 1

Gtrs. 1 & 3: w/ Riffs A & A1 (2 times)
Gtr. 2: w/ Rhy. Fig. 1 (2 times)
F#maj7add4 (Emaj7add4) ((Dmaj7add4))

first.

Verse

Gtr. 1: w/ Riff A (4 times)
Gtr. 2: w/ Rhy. Fig. 2A (4 times)
F#maj7add4 (Emaj7add4) ((Dmaj7add4))

3. On a moon spat-tered road in her par-rot re - bo - zo.

Gyp - sy Scot - ty is driv - ing his big, long, yel - low car.

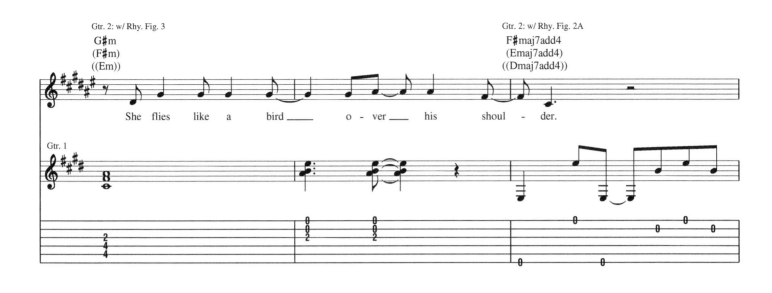

She flies like a bird ___ o - ver ___ his shoul - der.

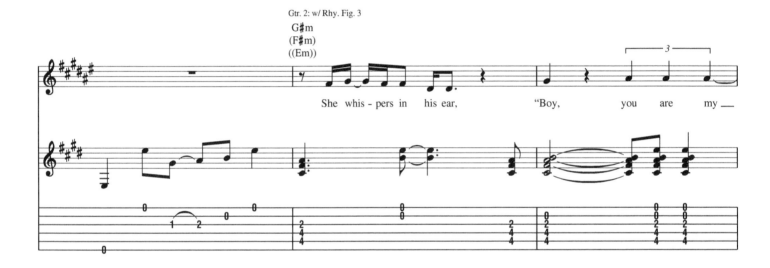

She whis - pers in his ear, "Boy, you are my ___

𝄋 Chorus

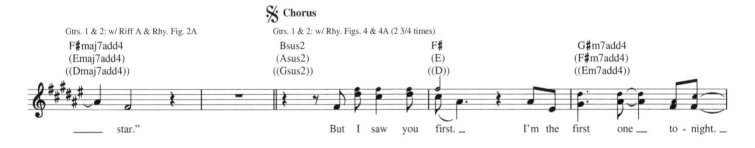

___ star." But I saw you first. ___ I'm the first one ___ to - night.

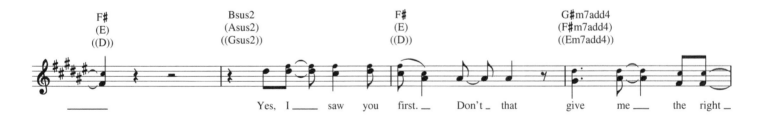

___ Yes, I ___ saw you first. Don't ___ that give me ___ the right

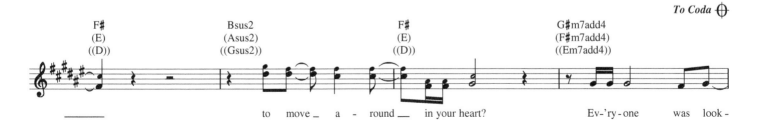

___ to move ___ a - round ___ in your heart? Ev - 'ry - one was look -

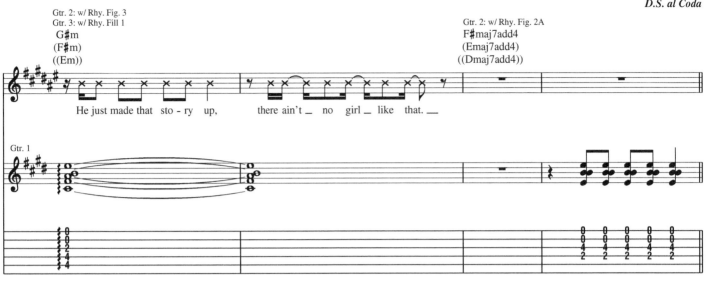

Coda

Outro

Lonely Ol' Night

Words and Music by John Mellencamp

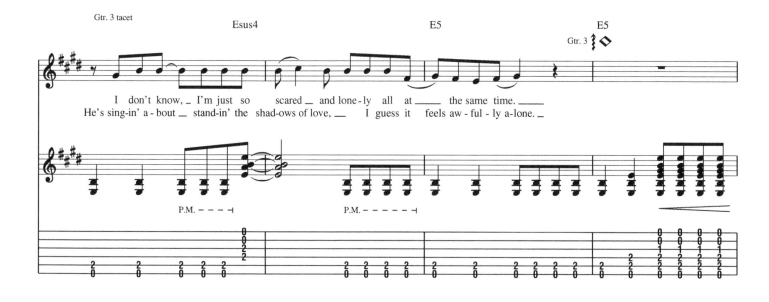

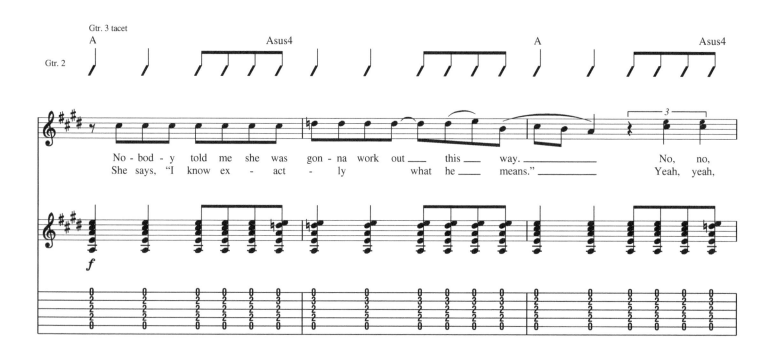

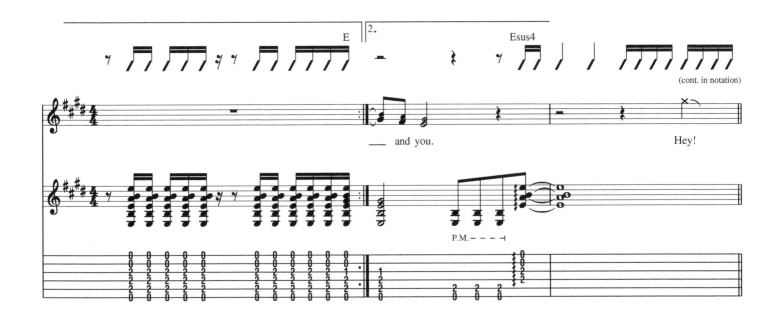

and you.   Hey!

(cont. in notation)

P.M.

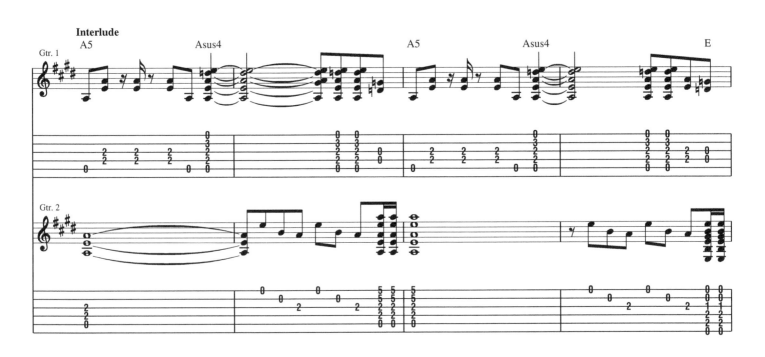

Interlude

Gtr. 1

Gtr. 2

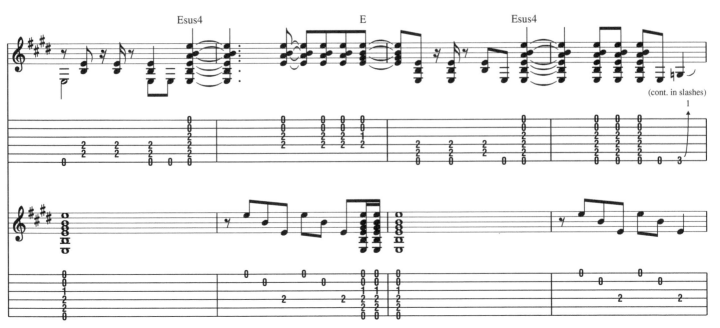

(cont. in slashes)

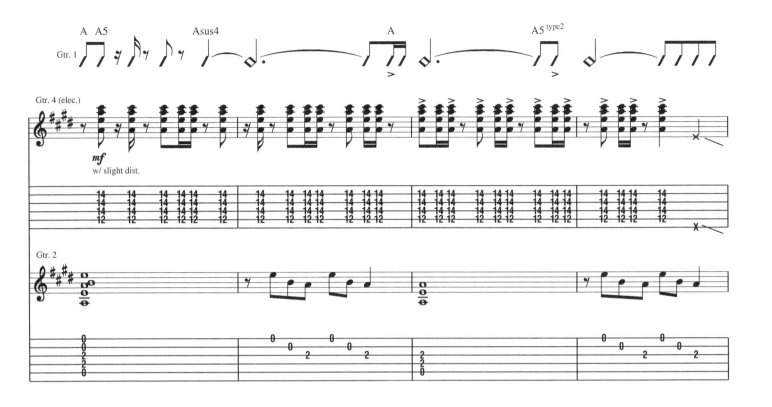

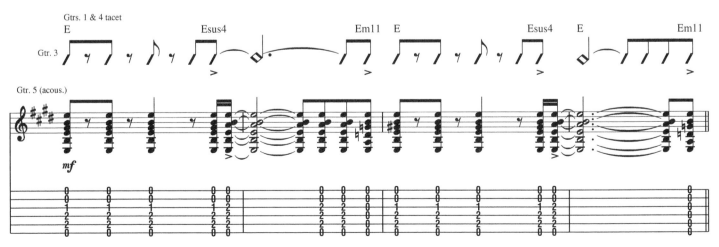

Paper in Fire

Words and Music by John Mellencamp

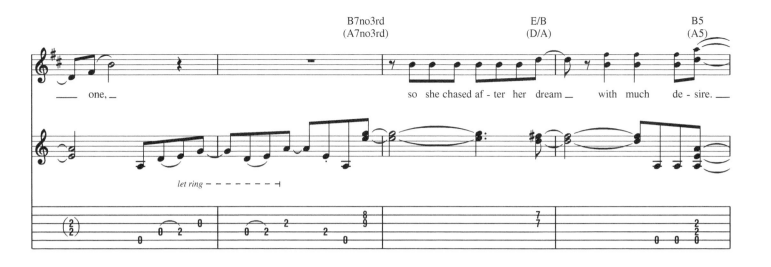

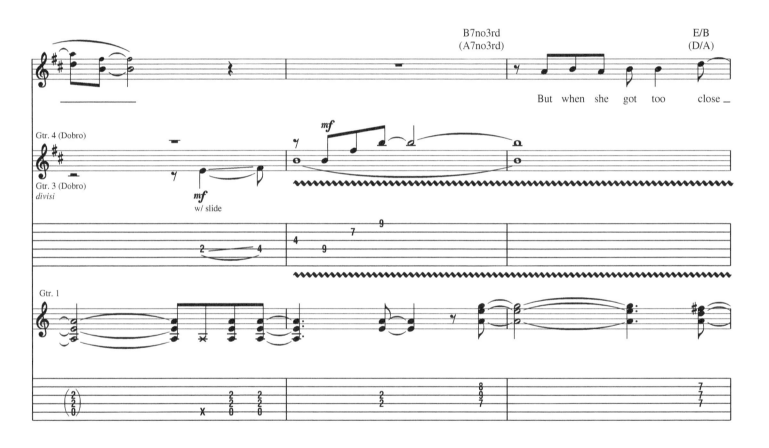

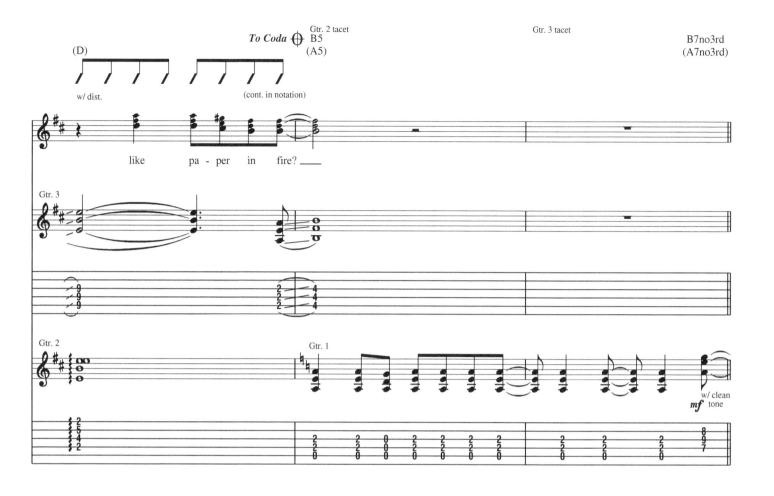

like pa-per in fire? ____

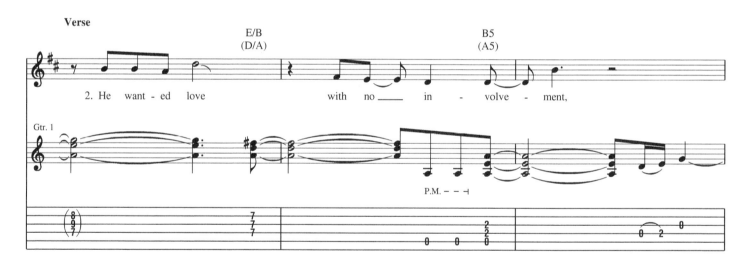

Verse

2. He want-ed love with no ____ in - volve - ment,

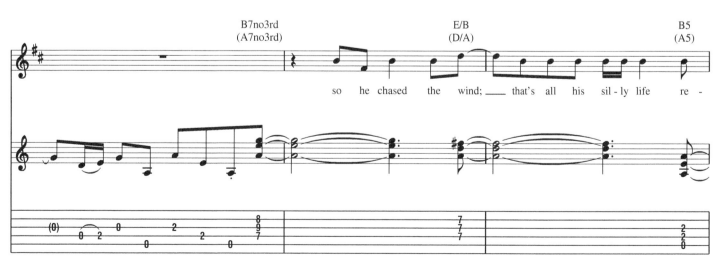

so he chased the wind; ____ that's all his sil - ly life re -

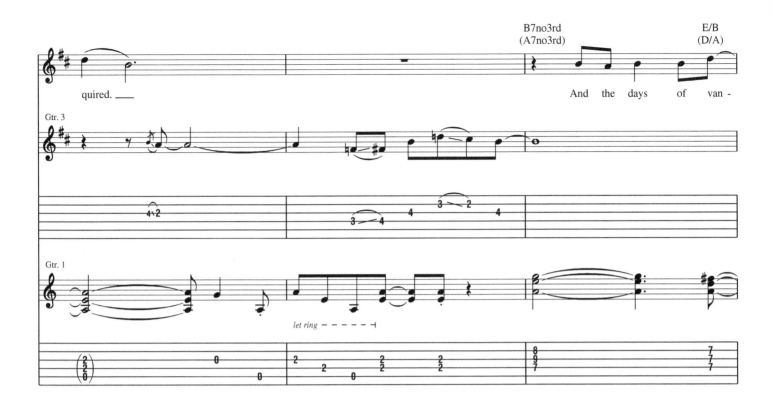

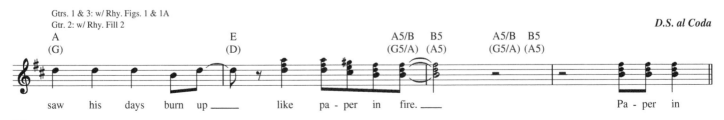

Chorus

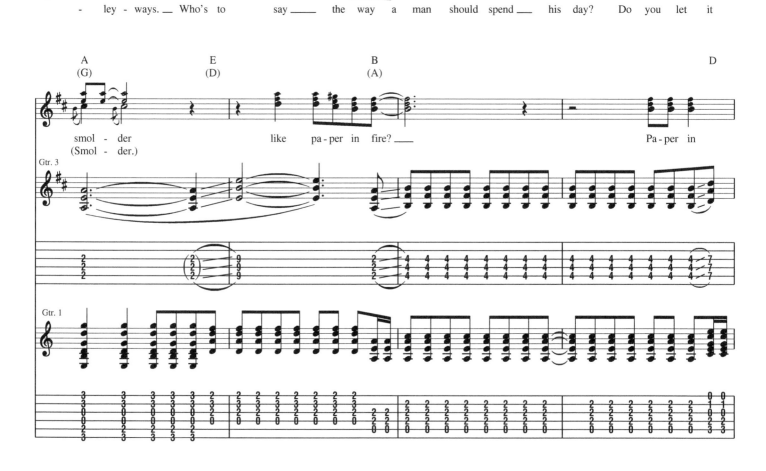

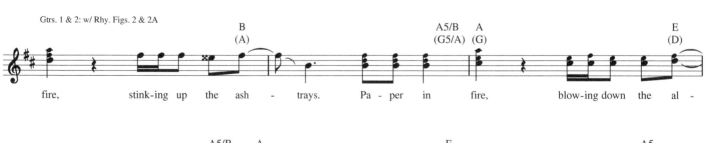

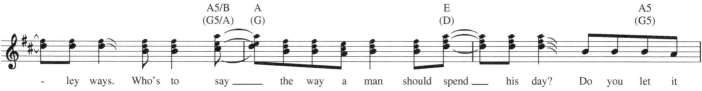

Peaceful World

Words and Music by John Mellencamp

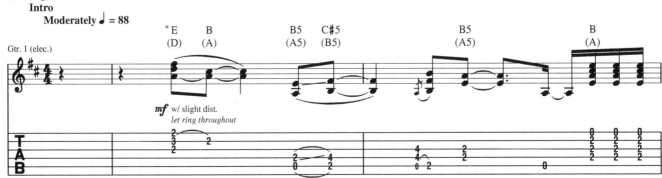

These are just words _ and words _ are o - kay. _ It's what you do _ and not what you say. If you're not

Chorus

Bkgd. Voc.: w/ Voc. Fig. 1
Gtr. 2 tacet

part of the fu - ture, then get out of the way. _ Come on, ba - by, take a ride _ with me. _ I'm up _

(Come on, ba - by, take a ride.

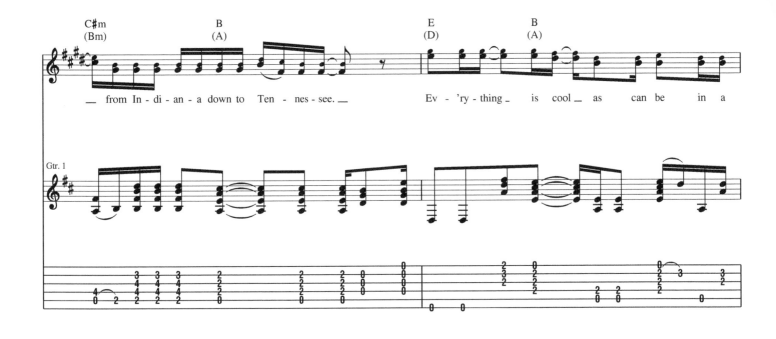

Verse

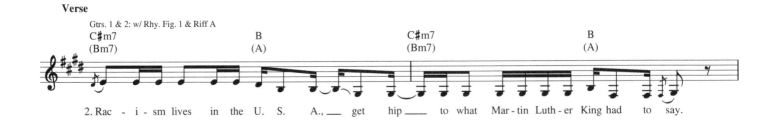

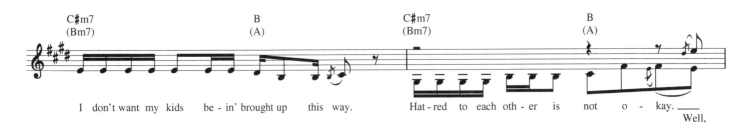

I'm not a preach-er, just a sing-er, son. __ I can see __ more work to be done. __ It's

what you do __ and not what you say. If you're not part of the fu - ture, then get out of the way. __

𝄉 Chorus

Bkgd. Voc.: w/ Voc. Fig. 1
Gtr. 1: w/ Rhy. Fig. 2 (2 times)   Bkgd. Voc.: w/ Voc. Fig. 2

Come on, ba - by, take a ride __ with me. __ I'm up __ from In - di - an - a down to Ten - nes - see. __

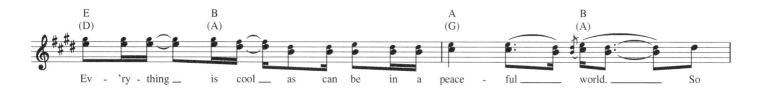

Ev - 'ry - thing __ is cool __ as can be in a peace - ful __ world. __ So

Bkgd. Voc.: w/ Voc. Fig. 1   Bkgd. Voc.: w/ Voc. Fig. 2

lay back the top and ride __ with me. __ I'm up __ from In - di - an - a down to Ten - nes - see. __

To Coda ⊕

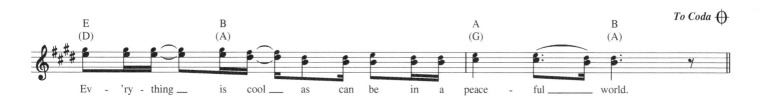

Ev - 'ry - thing __ is cool __ as can be in a peace - ful __ world.

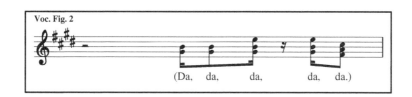

Voc. Fig. 2

(Da, da, da, da, da.)

Verse

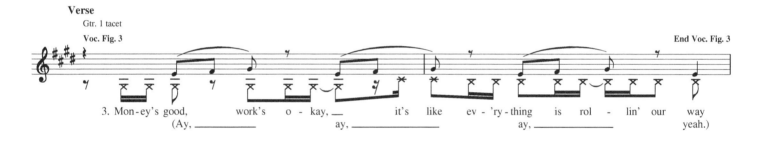

3. Mon-ey's good, work's o-kay, __ it's like ev - 'ry-thing is rol - lin' our way
(Ay, __ ay, __ ay, __ yeah.)

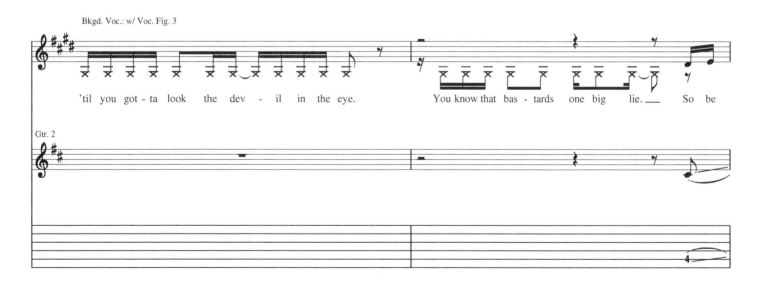

'til you got - ta look the dev - il in the eye. You know that bas - tards one big lie. __ So be

care - ful with your heart and what __ you love. Make sure __ that it __ was sent __ from a - bove. It's

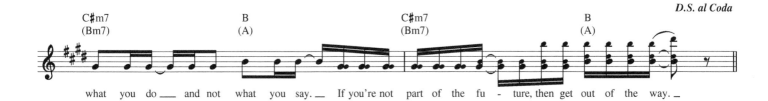

what you do ___ and not what you say. ___ If you're not part of the fu - ture, then get out of the way. ___

Coda

Outro

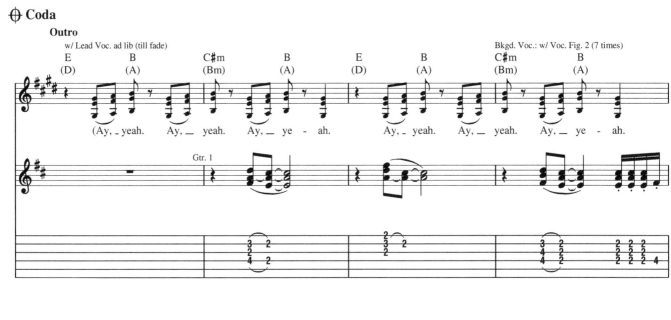

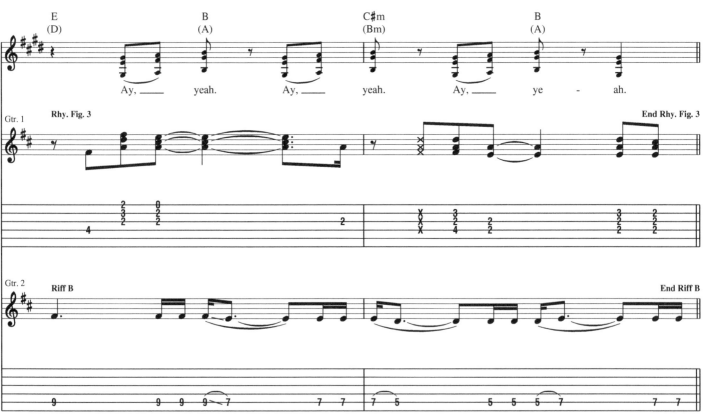

Pink Houses

Words and Music by John Mellencamp

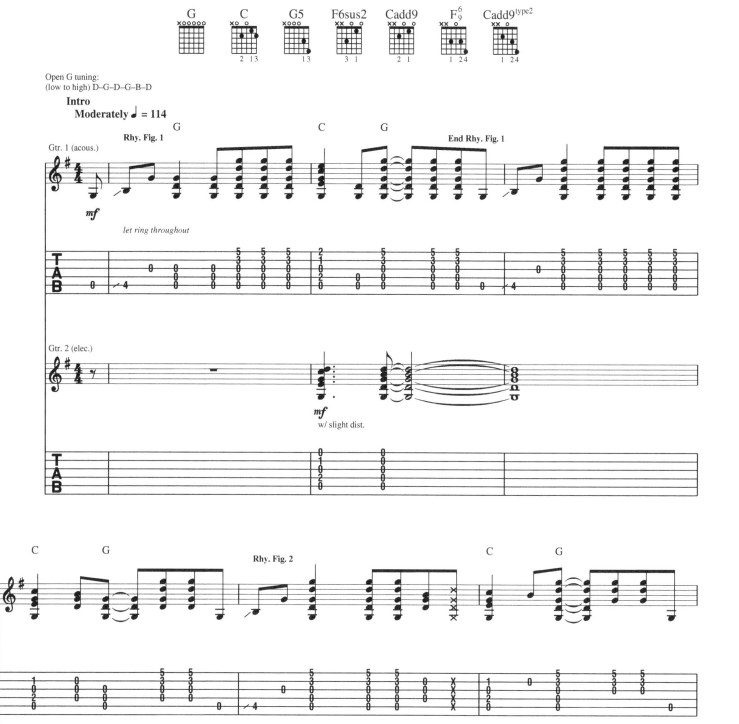

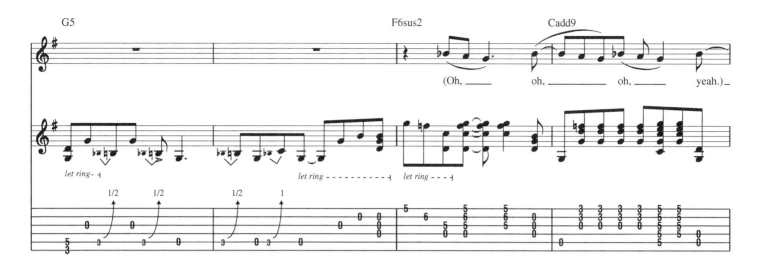

(Oh, ___ oh, ___ oh, ___ yeah.) ___

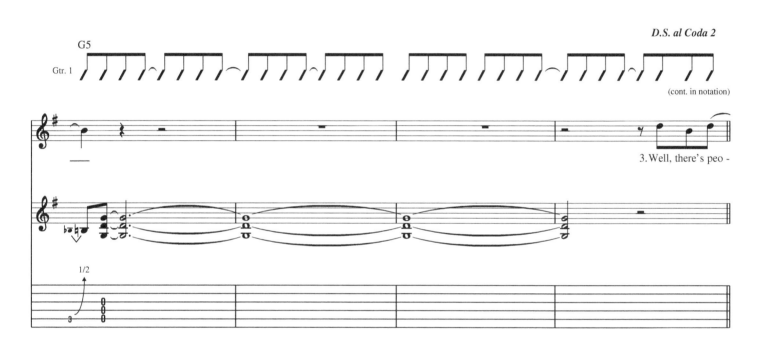

D.S. al Coda 2

(cont. in notation)

3. Well, there's peo -

⊕ Coda 2

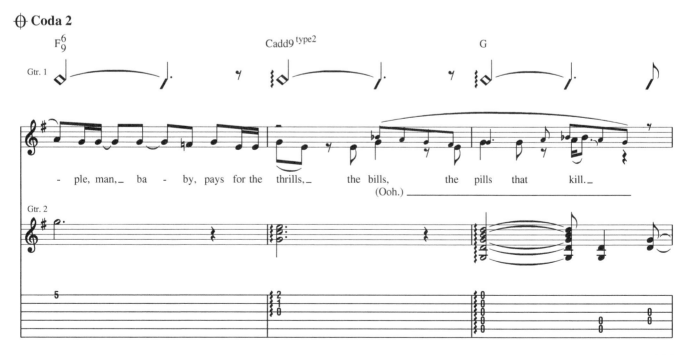

- ple, man,_ ba - by, pays for the thrills,_ the bills, the pills that kill.
(Ooh.) ___

R.O.C.K. in the U.S.A.
(A Salute to 60's Rock)

Words and Music by John Mellencamp

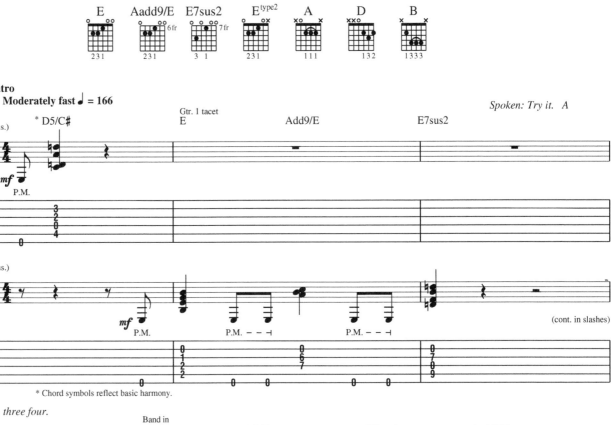

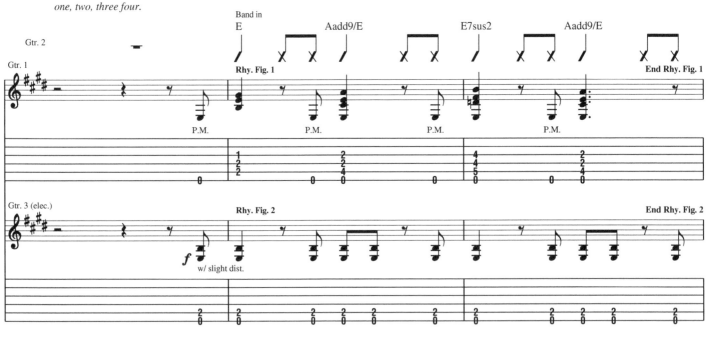

one, two, three four.

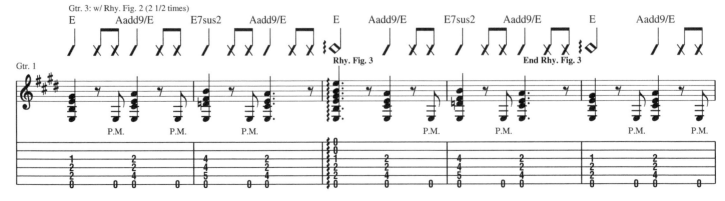

*Composite arrangement.

(cont. in notation)

2. Well, they

* Bass plays E, next 4 meas.

Verse

said good-bye ___ to their fam - 'lies,, said good-bye to their freinds. ___

With the pipe dreams in their heads and ver - y lit - tle mon - ey in ____ their hands..

____ Some are black ____ and some are white ____ and they

ain't too proud to sleep on your floor ____ to - night. ____ With the blind faith of Je - sus you

know that they ____ just might be rock - in' in the U. S.

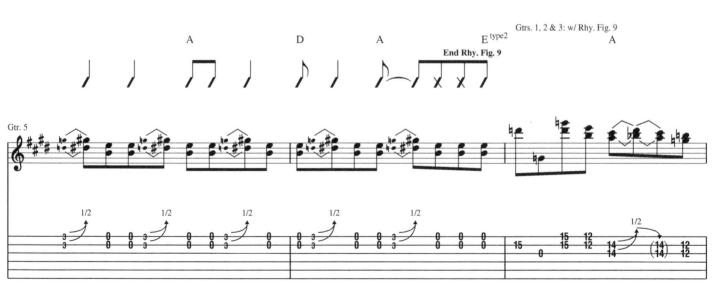

Verse

3. Voic-es from no-where and voic - es from the larg - er towns, ___

* Organ arr. for gtr.

filled ___ our head ___ full of dreams ___

___ and turned our world ___ up - side down. ___ There was

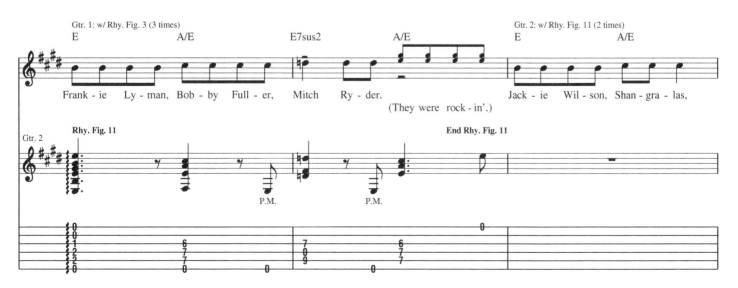

Frank - ie Ly - man, Bob - by Full - er, Mitch Ry - der.
(They were rock - in'.)
Jack - ie Wil - son, Shan - gra - las,

Young Ras - cals. Spot - light on Mar - tha Reeves. __ Let's don't for - get James
(They were rock - in'.)

Brown. ___ Rock - in' in the U. S. A. ___ Hey!

Outro-Chorus

Gtrs. 1, 2 & 3: w/ Rhy. Figs. 6 & 6A   Gtrs. 1, 2 & 3: w/ Rhy. Figs. 7 & 7A (3 times)

R. O. C. K. in the U. S. A. ___ R. ___ O. C. K. in the U. S. A. ___ R. ___

___ O. C. K. in the U. S. A. ___ R. ___ O. C. K. in the U. S. A. ___ R. ___

Repeat and fade

Gtrs. 1, 2 & 3: w/ Rhy. Figs. 7 & 7A (till fade)
Gtr. 5: w/ Rhy. Fig. 4A (till fade)

___ O. C. K. in the U. S. A. ___ R. ___ O. C. K. in the U. S. A. ___ R. ___

Small Town

Words and Music by John Mellencamp

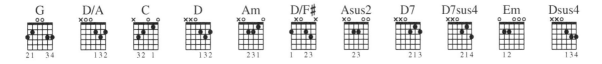

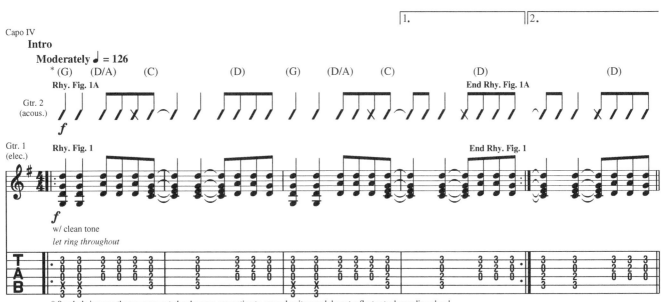

* Symbols in parentheses represent chord names respective to capoed guitars and do not reflect actual sounding chord.

Verse

1. Well, I was born in a small town. And I live in a small town.
2. Ed-u-cat-ed in a small town. Taught the fear of Je-sus in a small town.

** Symbols in parentheses represent chord names respective to capoed guitars.
Symbols above reflect actual sounding chord. Capoed fret is "0" in tab.

Prob-'ly die in a small town. Oh, those small com-mun-i-ties.
Used to day-dream in that small town. An-oth-er bor-ing ro-man-tic, that's me. But I've

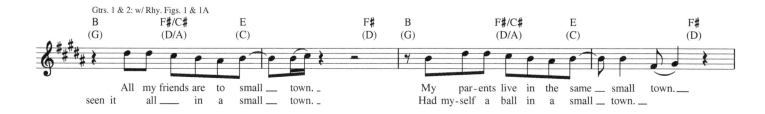

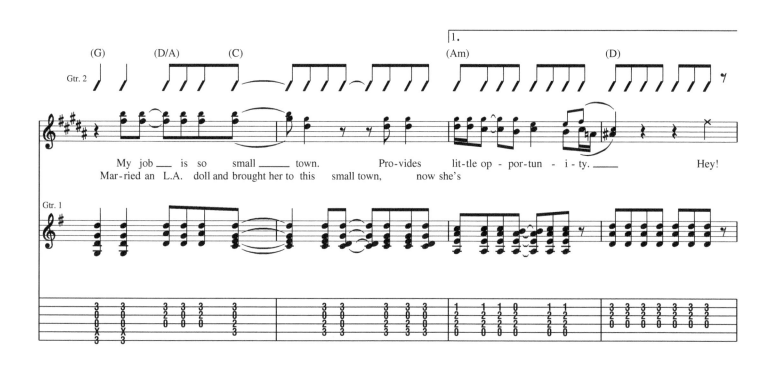

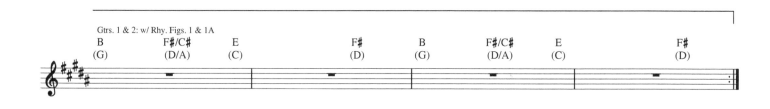

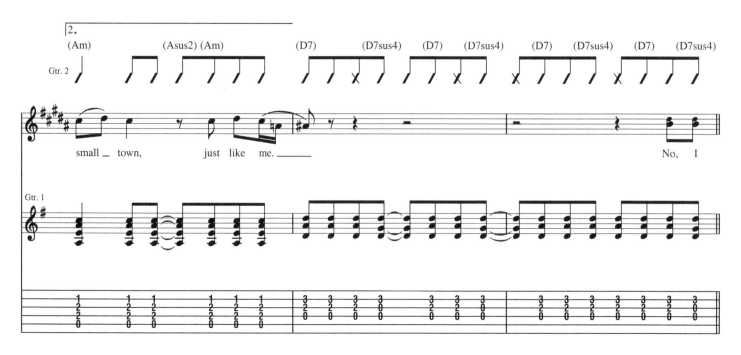

town.

And I ___ can breathe ___ in a small ___ town.

(Am)

Gon-na die ___ in a small ___ town.   Aw, that's prob-'ly where they'll bur - y me. ___   Yeah!

Outro

Gtrs. 1 & 2: w/ Rhy. Figs. 1 & 1A (3 1/2 times)
Gtr. 3 tacet

Ooh, ___ yeah, yeah, yeah. ___   Ha, be yeah.

Ooh,   yeah, yeah, yeah, yeah, yeah. ___   Yeah, yeah, yeah, yeah. ___

Gtr. 2

Gtr. 1

Wild Night

Words and Music by Van Morrison

the wild _____ nights _____ breeze _____ through your mind. _____
side the juke - box roars _____ just _____ like thun - der. _____

* Gtrs. 2 (slight dist.)
& 3 (clean)

(cont. in slashes)

* Composite arrangement.

Pre-Chorus

2nd & 3rd times, Gtr. 5: w/ Fill 1

And ev - 'ry - thing looks so com - plete _____ when you're

Gtr. 4
(dist.) **Rhy. Fill 1**   **End Rhy. Fill 1**

w/ slide

walk - ing down _ on the streets _____ and the wind _ catch - es your feet _

Fill 1
Gtr. 5

Wild ___ night ___ is call -

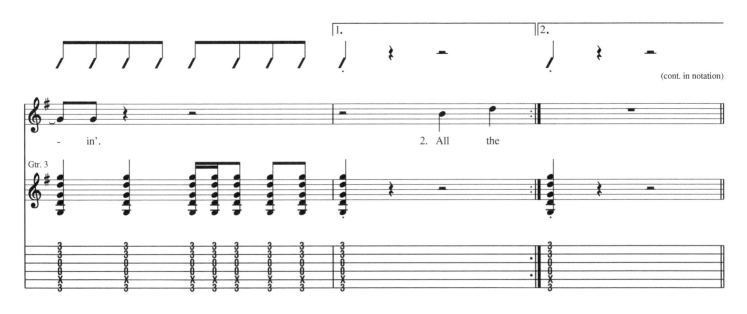

- in'.

2. All the

(cont. in notation)

Interlude

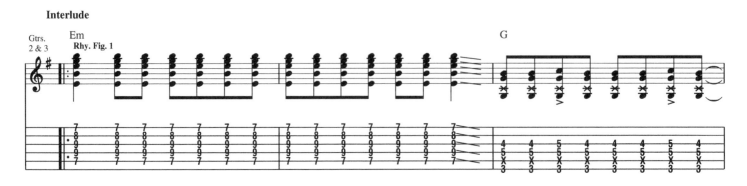

Your Life Is Now

Words and Music by John Mellencamp and George Green

Gtr. 1: Capo III

Intro

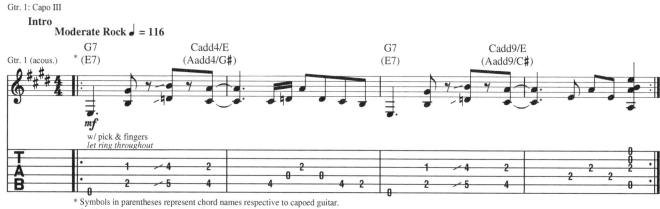

* Symbols in parentheses represent chord names respective to capoed guitar.
Symbols above reflect actual sounding chord. Capoed fret is "0" in tab.
Chord symbols reflect basic harmony.

Verse

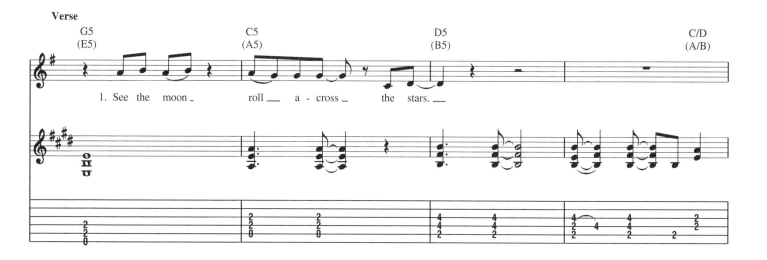

1. See the moon __ roll __ a-cross __ the stars. __

See the sea-sons turn __ like a heart. __

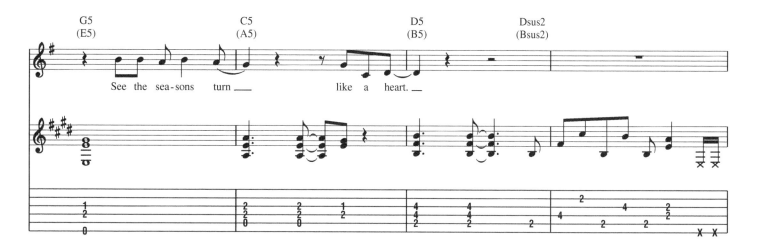

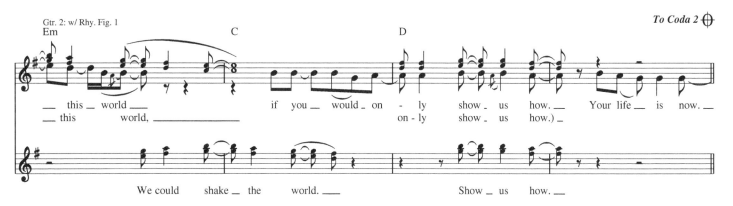

_ this _ world _   if you _ would on - ly show _ us how. _ Your life _ is now.
_ this world, _____   on - ly show _ us how.) _

We could shake _ the world. ___ Show _ us how. _

2. Would you teach your chil - dren to tell _ the truth? _

* Composite arrangement.

Would you take the high road if you could choose? _

138

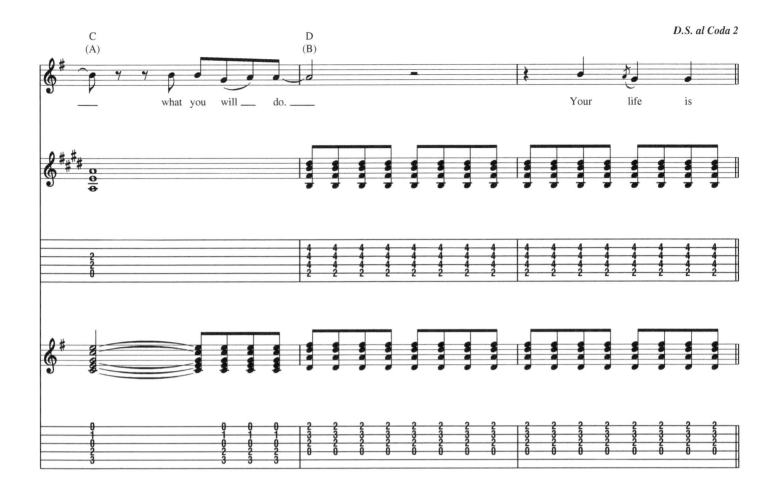

what you will do. Your life is

⊕ Coda 2

Gtr. 2: w/ Rhy. Fig. 2 (2 times)

Your life is now. Your life is now.

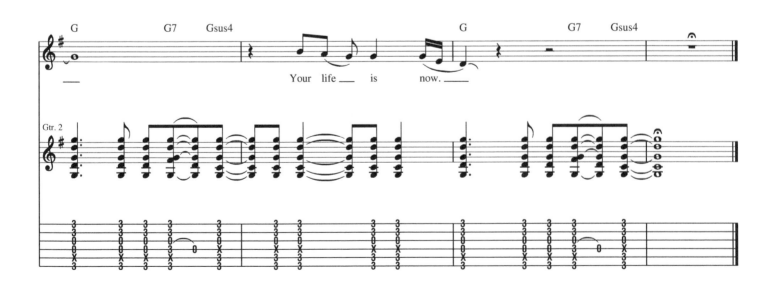

Your life is now.

Gtr. 2

Guitar Notation Legend

Guitar Music can be notated three different ways: on a *musical staff*, in *tablature*, and in *rhythm slashes*.

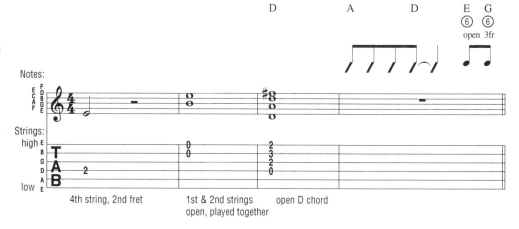

RHYTHM SLASHES are written above the staff. Strum chords in the rhythm indicated. Use the chord diagrams found at the top of the first page of the transcription for the appropriate chord voicings. Round noteheads indicate single notes.

THE MUSICAL STAFF shows pitches and rhythms and is divided by bar lines into measures. Pitches are named after the first seven letters of the alphabet.

TABLATURE graphically represents the guitar fingerboard. Each horizontal line represents a a string, and each number represents a fret.

Definitions for Special Guitar Notation

HALF-STEP BEND: Strike the note and bend up 1/2 step.

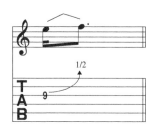

WHOLE-STEP BEND: Strike the note and bend up one step.

GRACE NOTE BEND: Strike the note and immediately bend up as indicated.

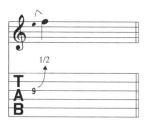

SLIGHT (MICROTONE) BEND: Strike the note and bend up 1/4 step.

BEND AND RELEASE: Strike the note and bend up as indicated, then release back to the original note. Only the first note is struck.

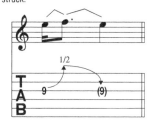

PRE-BEND: Bend the note as indicated, then strike it.

PRE-BEND AND RELEASE: Bend the note as indicated. Strike it and release the bend back to the original note.

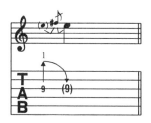

UNISON BEND: Strike the two notes simultaneously and bend the lower note up to the pitch of the higher.

VIBRATO: The string is vibrated by rapidly bending and releasing the note with the fretting hand.

WIDE VIBRATO: The pitch is varied to a greater degree by vibrating with the fretting hand.

HAMMER-ON: Strike the first (lower) note with one finger, then sound the higher note (on the same string) with another finger by fretting it without picking.

PULL-OFF: Place both fingers on the notes to be sounded. Strike the first note and without picking, pull the finger off to sound the second (lower) note.

LEGATO SLIDE: Strike the first note and then slide the same fret-hand finger up or down to the second note. The second note is not struck.

SHIFT SLIDE: Same as legato slide, except the second note is struck.

TRILL: Very rapidly alternate between the notes indicated by continuously hammering on and pulling off.

TAPPING: Hammer ("tap") the fret indicated with the pick-hand index or middle finger and pull off to the note fretted by the fret hand.

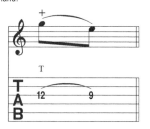

NATURAL HARMONIC: Strike the note while the fret-hand lightly touches the string directly over the fret indicated.

PINCH HARMONIC: The note is fretted normally and a harmonic is produced by adding the edge of the thumb or the tip of the index finger of the pick hand to the normal pick attack.

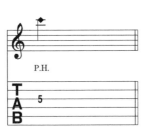

HARP HARMONIC: The note is fretted normally and a harmonic is produced by gently resting the pick hand's index finger directly above the indicated fret (in parentheses) while the pick hand's thumb or pick assists by plucking the appropriate string.

PICK SCRAPE: The edge of the pick is rubbed down (or up) the string, producing a scratchy sound.

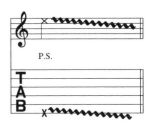

MUFFLED STRINGS: A percussive sound is produced by laying the fret hand across the string(s) without depressing, and striking them with the pick hand.

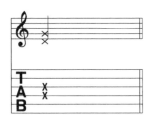

PALM MUTING: The note is partially muted by the pick hand lightly touching the string(s) just before the bridge.

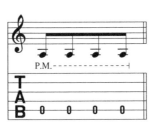

RAKE: Drag the pick across the strings indicated with a single motion.

TREMOLO PICKING: The note is picked as rapidly and continuously as possible.

ARPEGGIATE: Play the notes of the chord indicated by quickly rolling them from bottom to top.

VIBRATO BAR DIVE AND RETURN: The pitch of the note or chord is dropped a specified number of steps (in rhythm) then returned to the original pitch.

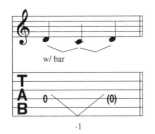

VIBRATO BAR SCOOP: Depress the bar just before striking the note, then quickly release the bar.

VIBRATO BAR DIP: Strike the note and then immediately drop a specified number of steps, then release back to the original pitch.

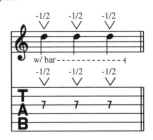

Additional Musical Definitions

 (accent) • Accentuate note (play it louder)

 (accent) • Accentuate note with great intensity

 (staccato) • Play the note short

⊓ • Downstroke

∨ • Upstroke

D.S. al Coda • Go back to the sign (𝄋), then play until the measure marked "*To Coda*," then skip to the section labelled "**Coda**."

D.C. al Fine • Go back to the beginning of the song and play until the measure marked "*Fine*" (end).

Rhy. Fig. • Label used to recall a recurring accompaniment pattern (usually chordal).

Riff • Label used to recall composed, melodic lines (usually single notes) which recur.

Fill • Label used to identify a brief melodic figure which is to be inserted into the arrangement.

Rhy. Fill • A chordal version of a Fill.

tacet • Instrument is silent (drops out).

 • Repeat measures between signs.

| 1. | 2. | • When a repeated section has different endings, play the first ending only the first time and the second ending only the second time.

NOTE: Tablature numbers in parentheses mean:
1. The note is being sustained over a system (note in standard notation is tied), or
2. The note is sustained, but a new articulation (such as a hammer-on, pull-off, slide or vibrato begins), or
3. The note is a barely audible "ghost" note (note in standard notation is also in parentheses).

RECORDED VERSIONS
The Best Note-For-Note Transcriptions Available

ALL BOOKS INCLUDE TABLATURE

00501	Adams, Bryan – Greatest Hits	$19.95
92015	Aerosmith – Greatest Hits	$22.95
00488	Aerosmith – Just Push Play	$19.95
00178	Alice in Chains – Acoustic	$19.95
94865	Alice in Chains – Dirt	$19.95
94925	Alice in Chains – Jar of Flies/Sap	$19.95
00387	Alice in Chains – Nothing Safe – The Best of the Box	$19.95
94932	Allman Brothers Band – Volume 1	$24.95
94933	Allman Brothers Band – Volume 2	$24.95
94934	Allman Brothers Band – Volume 3	$24.95
00513	American Hi-Fi	$19.95
94878	Atkins, Chet – Vintage Fingerstyle	$19.95
00418	Audio Adrenaline, Best of	$17.95
00366	Bad Company Original Anthology - Bk 1	$19.95
00367	Bad Company Original Anthology - Bk 2	$19.95
94929	Beatles: 1962-1966	$24.95
94930	Beatles: 1967-1970	$24.95
94880	Beatles – Abbey Road	$19.95
00110	Beatles – Book 1 (White Album)	$19.95
94832	Beatles – For Acoustic Guitar	$19.95
50140	Beatles – Guitar Book	$19.95
94863	Beatles – Sgt. Pepper's Lonely Hearts Club Band	$19.95
00397	Beck – Midnite Vultures	$19.95
94884	Benson, George – Best of	$19.95
92385	Berry, Chuck	$19.95
92200	Black Sabbath – We Sold Our Soul for Rock 'N' Roll	$19.95
00305	Blink 182 – Dude Ranch	$19.95
00389	Blink 182 – Enema of the State	$19.95
00523	Blink 182 – Take Off Your Pants & Jacket	$19.95
00028	Blue Oyster Cult – Cult Classics	$19.95
00168	Buchanan, Roy – Collection	$19.95
90491	Bowie, David – Best of	$19.95
90451	Buckley, Jeff – Collection	$24.95
00364	Cake – Songbook	$19.95
90293	Chapman, Steven Curtis – Best of	$19.95
90043	Cheap Trick – Best of	$19.95
00171	Chicago – Definitive Guitar Collection	$22.95
90415	Clapton Chronicles – Best of Eric Clapton	$18.95
90393	Clapton, Eric – Selections from Blues	$19.95
90074	Clapton, Eric – The Cream of Clapton	$24.95
90010	Clapton, Eric – From the Cradle	$19.95
60139	Clapton, Eric – Journeyman	$19.95
94869	Clapton, Eric – Unplugged	$22.95
94896	Clapton, Eric/John Mayall – Bluesbreakers	$19.95
90162	Clash, Best of	$19.95
90494	Coldplay – Parachutes	$19.95
94940	Counting Crows – August & Everything After	$19.95
94840	Cream – Disraeli Gears	$19.95
90401	Creed – Human Clay	$19.95
90352	Creed – My Own Prison	$19.95
90484	dc Talk – Intermission: The Greatest Hits	$19.95
90289	Deep Purple, Best of	$17.95
90384	Di Franco, Ani – Best of	$19.95
90322	Di Franco, Ani – Little Plastic Castle	$19.95
90380	Di Franco, Ani – Up Up Up Up Up Up	$19.95
95382	Dire Straits – Sultans of Swing	$19.95
90347	Doors, The – Anthology	$22.95
90348	Doors, The – Essential Guitar Collection	$16.95
90524	Etheridge, Melissa – Skin	$19.95
90349	Eve 6	$19.95
90496	Everclear, Best of	$19.95
90515	Extreme II – Pornograffitti	$19.95
90323	Fastball – All the Pain Money Can Buy	$19.95
90235	Foo Fighters – The Colour and the Shape	$19.95

00690394	Foo Fighters – There Is Nothing Left to Lose	$19.95
00690222	G3 Live – Satriani, Vai, Johnson	$22.95
00690536	Garbage – Beautiful Garbage	$19.95
00690438	Genesis Guitar Anthology	$19.95
00690338	Goo Goo Dolls – Dizzy Up the Girl	$19.95
00690114	Guy, Buddy – Collection Vol. A-J	$22.95
00690193	Guy, Buddy – Collection Vol. L-Y	$22.95
00694798	Harrison, George – Anthology	$19.95
00692930	Hendrix, Jimi – Are You Experienced?	$24.95
00692931	Hendrix, Jimi – Axis: Bold As Love	$22.95
00694944	Hendrix, Jimi – Blues	$24.95
00692932	Hendrix, Jimi – Electric Ladyland	$24.95
00690218	Hendrix, Jimi – First Rays of the New Rising Sun	$27.95
00690017	Hendrix, Jimi – Woodstock	$24.95
00660029	Holly, Buddy	$19.95
00690054	Hootie & The Blowfish – Cracked Rear View	$19.95
00690457	Incubus – Make Yourself	$19.95
00690544	Incubus – Morningview	$19.95
00690136	Indigo Girls – 1200 Curfews	$22.95
00694833	Joel, Billy – For Guitar	$19.95
00694912	Johnson, Eric – Ah Via Musicom	$19.95
00694799	Johnson, Robert – At the Crossroads	$19.95
00690271	Johnson, Robert – The New Transcriptions	$24.95
00699131	Joplin, Janis – Best of	$19.95
00693185	Judas Priest – Vintage Hits	$19.95
00690444	King, B.B. and Eric Clapton – Riding with the King	$19.95
00690339	Kinks, The – Best of	$19.95
00690279	Liebert, Ottmar + Luna Negra – Opium Highlights	$19.95
00694755	Malmsteen, Yngwie – Rising Force	$19.95
00694956	Marley, Bob – Legend	$19.95
00694945	Marley, Bob – Songs of Freedom	$24.95
00690283	McLachlan, Sarah – Best of	$19.95
00690382	McLachlan, Sarah – Mirrorball	$19.95
00690442	Matchbox 20 – Mad Season	$19.95
00690239	Matchbox 20 – Yourself or Someone Like You	$19.95
00694952	Megadeth – Countdown to Extinction	$19.95
00690391	Megadeth – Risk	$19.95
00694951	Megadeth – Rust in Peace	$22.95
00690495	Megadeth – The World Needs a Hero	$19.95
00690040	Miller, Steve, Band – Greatest Hits	$19.95
00690448	MxPx – The Ever Passing Moment	$19.95
00690189	Nirvana – From the Muddy Banks of the Wishkah	$19.95
00694913	Nirvana – In Utero	$19.95
00694883	Nirvana – Nevermind	$19.95
00690026	Nirvana – Unplugged™ in New York	$19.95
00690121	Oasis – (What's the Story) Morning Glory	$19.95
00690358	Offspring, The – Americana	$19.95
00690485	Offspring, The – Conspiracy of One	$19.95
00690203	Offspring, The – Smash	$18.95
00694847	Osbourne, Ozzy – Best of	$22.95
00694830	Osbourne, Ozzy – No More Tears	$19.95
00690538	Oysterhead – The Grand Pecking Order	$19.95
00694855	Pearl Jam – Ten	$19.95
00690439	Perfect Circle, A – Mer De Noms	$19.95
00690176	Phish – Billy Breathes	$22.95
00690424	Phish – Farmhouse	$19.95
00690240	Phish – Hoist	$19.95
00690331	Phish – Story of the Ghost	$19.95
00690428	Pink Floyd – Dark Side of the Moon	$19.95
00690456	P.O.D. – The Fundamental Elements of Southtown	$19.95
00693864	Police, The – Best of	$19.95

00690299	Presley, Elvis – Best of Elvis: The King of Rock 'n' Roll	$19.95
00694975	Queen – Greatest Hits	$24.95
00694910	Rage Against the Machine	$19.95
00690395	Rage Against the Machine – The Battle of Los Angeles	$19.95
00690145	Rage Against the Machine – Evil Empire	$19.95
00690478	Rage Against the Machine – Renegades	$19.95
00690426	Ratt – Best of	$19.95
00690055	Red Hot Chili Peppers – Bloodsugarsexmagik	$19.95
00690379	Red Hot Chili Peppers – Californication	$19.95
00690090	Red Hot Chili Peppers – One Hot Minute	$22.95
00694899	R.E.M. – Automatic for the People	$19.95
00690014	Rolling Stones – Exile on Main Street	$24.95
00690135	Rush, Otis – Collection	$19.95
00690502	Saliva – Every Six Seconds	$19.95
00690031	Santana's Greatest Hits	$19.95
00120123	Shepherd, Kenny Wayne – Trouble Is	$19.95
00690419	Slipknot	$19.95
00690530	Slipknot – Iowa	$19.95
00690330	Social Distortion – Live at the Roxy	$19.95
00690385	Sonicflood	$19.95
00694957	Stewart, Rod – Unplugged...And Seated	$22.95
00690021	Sting – Fields of Gold	$19.95
00690519	Sum 41 – All Killer No Filler	$19.95
00690425	System of a Down	$19.95
00690531	System of a Down – Toxicity	$19.95
00694824	Taylor, James – Best of	$16.95
00692238	Third Eye Blind	$19.95
00690403	Third Eye Blind – Blue	$19.95
00690295	Tool – Aenima	$19.95
00690039	Vai, Steve – Alien Love Secrets	$24.95
00690343	Vai, Steve – Flex-able Leftovers	$19.95
00660137	Vai, Steve – Passion & Warfare	$24.95
00690392	Vai, Steve – The Ultra Zone	$19.95
00690370	Vaughan, Stevie Ray and Double Trouble – The Real Deal: Greatest Hits Volume 2	$22.95
00690455	Vaughan, Stevie Ray – Blues at Sunrise	$19.95
00690116	Vaughan, Stevie Ray – Guitar Collection	$24.95
00660136	Vaughan, Stevie Ray – In Step	$19.95
00660058	Vaughan, Stevie Ray – Lightnin' Blues 1983-1987	$24.95
00690417	Vaughan, Stevie Ray – Live at Carnegie Hall	$19.95
00694835	Vaughan, Stevie Ray – The Sky Is Crying	$22.95
00690015	Vaughan, Stevie Ray – Texas Flood	$19.95
00120026	Walsh, Joe – Look What I Did...	$24.95
00694789	Waters, Muddy – Deep Blues	$24.95
00690071	Weezer	$19.95
00690516	Weezer (The Green Album)	$19.95
00690286	Weezer – Pinkerton	$19.95
00690447	Who, The – Best of	$24.95
00690320	Williams, Dar – Best of	$17.95
00690319	Wonder, Stevie – Some of the Best	$17.95
00690443	Zappa, Frank – Hot Rats	$19.95

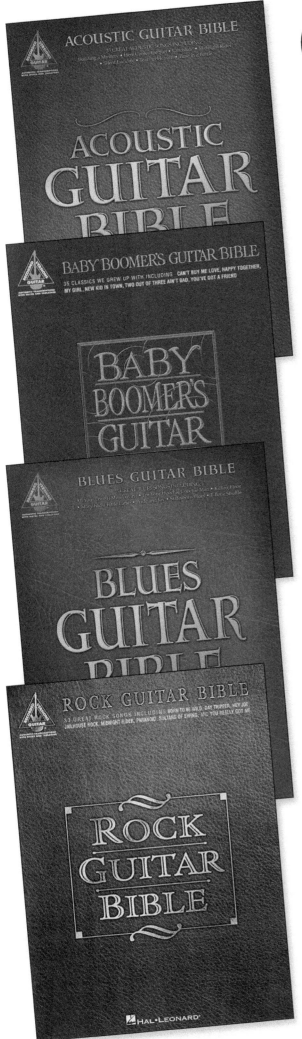

GUITAR BIBLES
from
HAL•LEONARD®

Hal Leonard proudly presents the Guitar Bible series.
Each volume contains great songs in authentic,
note-for-note transcriptions with lyrics and tablature. $19.95 each

ACOUSTIC GUITAR BIBLE

35 acoustic classics: Angie • Building a Mystery • Change the World • Dust in the Wind • Here Comes the Sun • Hold My Hand • Iris • Maggie May • Southern Cross • Tears in Heaven • Wild World • You Were Meant for Me • and more.
_____00690432..$19.95

BABY BOOMER'S GUITAR BIBLE

35 songs: Angie • Can't Buy Me Love • Happy Together • Hey Jude • Imagine • Laughing • Longer • My Girl • New Kid in Town • Rebel, Rebel • Wild Thing • and more.
_____00690412..$19.95

BLUES GUITAR BIBLE

35 blues tunes: Boom Boom • Everyday (I Have the Blues) • Hide Away • I Can't Quit You Baby • I'm Your Hoochie Coochie Man • Killing Floor • Pride and Joy • Sweet Little Angel • The Thrill Is Gone • and more.
_____00690437..$19.95

BLUES-ROCK GUITAR BIBLE

35 songs: Cross Road Blues (Crossroads) • Hide Away • The House Is Rockin' • Love Struck Baby • Move It On Over • Piece of My Heart • Statesboro Blues • You Shook Me • more.
_____00690450..$19.95

COUNTRY GUITAR BIBLE

35 country classics: Ain't Goin' Down ('Til the Sun Comes Up) • Blue Eyes Crying in the Rain • Boot Scootin' Boogie • Friends in Low Places • I'm So Lonesome I Could Cry • T-R-O-U-B-L-E • and more.
_____00690465..$19.95

FOLK-ROCK GUITAR BIBLE

35 songs: At Seventeen • Blackbird • Fire and Rain • Happy Together • Leaving on a Jet Plane • Our House • Time in a Bottle • Turn! Turn! Turn! • You've Got a Friend • more.
_____00690464..$19.95

HARD ROCK GUITAR BIBLE

35 songs: Ballroom Blitz • Bang a Gong • Barracuda • Living After Midnight • Rock You like a Hurricane • School's Out • Welcome to the Jungle • You Give Love a Bad Name • more.
_____00690453..$19.95

JAZZ GUITAR BIBLE

31 songs: Body and Soul • In a Sentimental Mood • My Funny Valentine • Nuages • Satin Doll • So What • Star Dust • Take Five • Tangerine • Yardbird Suite • and more.
_____00690466..$19.95

NU METAL GUITAR BIBLE

25 edgy metal hits: Aenema • Black • Edgecrusher • Last Resort • People of the Sun • Schism • Sleep Now in the Fire • Southtown • Take a Look Around • Toxicity • Your Disease • Youth of the Nation • and more.
_____00690569..$19.95

POP/ROCK GUITAR BIBLE

35 pop hits: Change the World • Heartache Tonight • Hold My Hand • Money for Nothing • Mony, Mony • More Than Words • Pink Houses • Smooth • Summer of '69 • 3 AM • What I Like About You • and more.
_____00690517..$19.95

R&B GUITAR BIBLE

35 R&B classics: Brick House • Fire • I Got You (I Feel Good) • Love Rollercoaster • Shining Star • Sir Duke • Super Freak • and more.
_____00690452..$19.95

ROCK GUITAR BIBLE

33 songs: All Day and All of the Night • Born to Be Wild • Day Tripper • Gloria • Hey Joe • Jailhouse Rock • Money • Paranoid • Sultans of Swing • Walk This Way • You Really Got Me • more!
_____00690313..$19.95

ROCKABILLY GUITAR BIBLE

30 songs from artists such as Elvis, Buddy Holly and the Brian Setzer Orchestra: Blue Suede Shoes • Hello Mary Lou • Peggy Sue • Rock This Town • Travelin' Man • and more.
_____00690570..$19.95

SOUL GUITAR BIBLE

33 songs: Groovin' • I've Been Loving You Too Long • Let's Get It On • My Girl • Respect • Theme from Shaft • Soul Man • and more.
_____00690506..$19.95

Prices, contents, and availability subject to change without notice.

www.halleonard.com   0402